W9-CAB-312

WITCHES
of The World

WITCHES
of The World

Diane Canwell & Jonathan Sutherland

CHARTWELL
BOOKS, INC.

Published in 2007 by
CHARTWELL BOOKS, INC.
A division of BOOK SALES, INC.
114 Northfield Avenue
Edison, New Jersey 08837
USA

**Copyright © 2007 Regency
House Publishing Limited**
Niall House
24–26 Boulton Road
Stevenage, Hertfordshire
SG1 4QX, UK

For all editorial enquiries please contact
Regency House Publishing at
www.regencyhousepublishing.com

All rights reserved. No part of this book
may be reproduced in any form or by any
electronic or mechanical means, including
information, storage and retrieval systems,
without permission in writing from the
publisher.

ISBN-13: 978-0-7858-2283-7

ISBN-10: 0-7858-2283-6

Printed in China

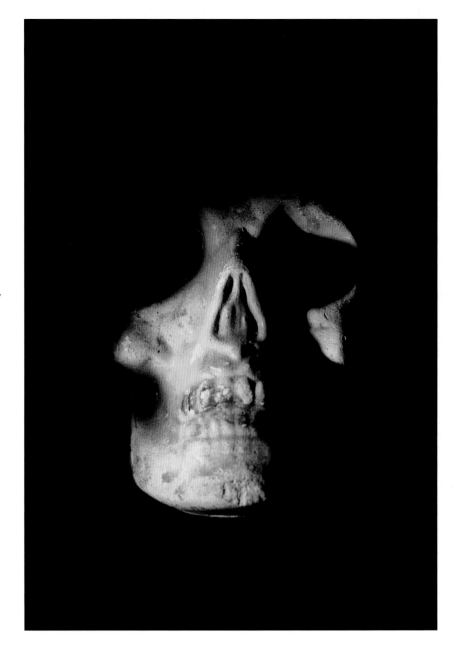

CONTENTS

INTRODUCTION

The words witch and witchcraft have been in use for over 1,000 years, although today our understanding of the words have more to do with magic and sorcery. But during the 16th and 17th centuries, particularly in Europe and North America, the words had altogether different connotations.

Had the stereotypical view of the witch as an old crone been different – that is of an old woman leaning on a staff and mumbling to herself as she shuffled along – then the horrors of the period 1450–1750 may never have occurred. Untold numbers of crimes were committed against innocent old women, under the guise of concern for their immortal souls, in a period that would shake the principles of honour and justice to their very roots.

It took nearly two centuries in Europe for some 200,000 witches to be mutilated, burned or strangled, but the numbers involved, considering the extended period over which the events took place, pale into insignificance

compared with the slaughter perpetrated in the 20th century during the Nazi Holocaust. Unlike the latter, the hunting of witches was not purposeful and systematic, and witches were burned in ones and twos over many decades. The killings were not restricted to any particular areas, but happened in nearly every town and village across the European continent.

Witchcraft means many different things to different peoples around the world, but the blanket use of the word

has only served to obscure its original meaning. To the theologians, judges and lawyers of the witch-hunt period, witchcraft meant only one thing: that a pact had been made with the Devil to do evil. For Christians, therefore, witchcraft could be nothing other than a heresy, and action to eradicate it was accordingly justified.

Cotton Mather (1663–1728), a minister of Boston's North Church in Massachusetts, and a firm believer in witchcraft wrote: 'So horrid and hellish is the crime of witchcraft that were God's thoughts as our thoughts, or God's way as our ways, it could be no other but unpardonable.'

ABOVE LEFT: Cotton Mather, whose name is inextricably linked with the witch trials in America.

OPPOSITE: This photograph, taken in 1901, shows an innocent old woman at her spinning wheel, her dog at her side, which to some, by reason of past stereotyping, might suggest a witch.

Mather, like many others, believed that witchcraft meant being in league with the Devil, and that mischievous or malicious acts were being performed in his name. Underlying this was a lingering belief in sorcery and magic, both of which had existed since pagan times; even when Christianity became the dominant religion in Europe, elements of the old pagan religion were never wholly obliterated. The association of witchcraft with heresy reached a fever pitch from the late medieval period onwards, when accusations of witchcraft were frequently combined with other heresies, as was the case with the Cathars of south-western France.

At first, witchcraft was seen as a form of natural magic, a lingering remnant of a pagan past. Sorcery and magic were worldwide phenomena and as old as humanity itself, their original purpose being to overcome and control the forces of nature, which mankind as yet only imperfectly understood. But

An illustration from The Lancashire Witches, *by William Harrison Ainsworth, in which Nicholas Ashton is catching women suspected of practising witchcraft.*

Meanwhile, vestiges of the older, more shamanistic religions persisted in Europe, in Africa, across Asia and in both North and South America. The invocation of spirits, the belief in demons, and the efficacy of rituals that would ensure the fertility of man, his livestock and crops, together with the use of charms, talismans and curses, continued to persist

In Europe, prior to the 14th century, witchcraft was only punishishable by death if injury to another had taken

LEFT: St. Thomas Aquinas.

BELOW: Gargoyles, such as this on the 14th-century Church of St.-Jean in Lyon, were often depicted as demons and grotesques.

place. Otherwise, it was treated in much the same way as prostitution. But after ecclesiastical law came to be applied, punishment became more frequent and severe. Meanwhile, Christians were happy to ignore another kind of

formal, ostensibly God-inspired religions, that would develop and deliver a catechism of required beliefs. The views of St. Augustine of Hippo (354–430) on the difference between magic and miracle were crucial in the early Church's fight against paganism and would become important during the later denunciations of witches, as would the teachings of St. Thomas Aquinas (c.1225–1274), another formulator of Christian doctrine, who held similar implacable views.

'witchcraft', when it came in the guise of miracles performed by saints. Saints, in this context, were seen as having successfully overcome a trap laid for them by Satan.

The *Malleus Maleficarum*, first published in 1486 and one of the most infamous books ever written, served as a guide to identifying witches, so that they could be prosecuted and despatched. Parallels can be seen in the later witch-hunt craze, which would lead to apparently god-fearing people denouncing their neighbours. What traits did these so-called witches possess? What evil purpose lay behind their use of common plants and everyday objects? How could one protect oneself from them? Who were the witch-hunters and how did they identify and deal with witches? How were confessions forced from the accused and, after they had been made to implicate other innocents, what was their fate?

LEFT: A photograph of an African witch doctor, taken c.1920.

OPPOSITE: Charms, fetishes and herbs on sale in a market in La Paz, Bolivia, used to protect against evil spells.

Mass hysteria is a recurring theme running through this book. It tells of a period when midwives, herbalists, quacks and the mentally impaired, along with troublesome neighbours and harmless eccentrics, were confronted by torture and a hideous death. This frenzy of suspicion spared none, from the poor and homeless to members of the higher echelons of society. It was a veritable epidemic of persecution, and no one could prevent it from spreading like wildfire throughout the world.

The persecution of witches came to an end at different times in different places, and reveals the full extent of the terror. In Holland it was 1610, England 1684, America 1692, Scotland 1712, France 1745, Germany 1775, Switzerland 1782 and Poland 1793. As societies began to mature, the subject of witchcraft gradually began to disappear from people's minds.

The delusions of witchcraft would have continued for even longer, had it not been for those who sought actively to remove them. A very few admitted their guilt, but most denied it to the bitter end, cursing their accusers as they were dragged to their deaths at the stake.

CHAPTER ONE
THE WITCH-HUNT CRAZE

*W*itchcraft was a matter that concerned not only Europe but other continents during the 16th and 17th centuries. Peasants worried about their crops and animals, priests were alert to signs that the Devil was dwelling in their parishioners, medical quacks were only too eager to profit from the fear of evil women and cunning men, and the judiciary was

BELOW & OPPOSITE: Many innocent men and women where caught and tried for witchcraft. They were invariably tortured to gain a confession, and many died during the process.

zealous in its attempts to crush the influence of diabolism.

The word 'witch' described a person who used charms and spells, assisted by evil spirits, to accomplish their wicked intent. But it also came to encompass a great many other so-called supernatural phenomena, when people who allegedly could change their shape, those suspected of being in league with the Devil, and almost certainly those who took part in strange nocturnal rituals, were also included.

Notions of what it meant to be a witch probably came from Christian Byzantium towards the end of the ninth century, and told of men making pacts with Satan after he had promised them untold riches in return for their immortal souls. It was also around this time that the first manifestations of the Witches' Sabbat began to appear, described as nocturnal assemblies of witches, who, it was believed, rode through the air to arrive at these meetings. The purpose of the Sabbats was to pay homage to their true master, the Devil, for whom witches had renounced their Christianity and their baptismal vows and to whom they had

LEFT: The clergy wholeheartedly sanctioned the hunt for witches.

BELOW: William Byg was arrested for using a crystal ball to find criminals.

surrendered themselves body and soul. They now existed solely to do the Devil's bidding, performing the tasks and duties that, for some reason, he could not do himself. By the time these ideas came to be common currency, an elaborate theological background surrounding the practice and purpose of witchcraft had been devised.

In 1390 the London soothsayer, John Berking, was arrested and found guilty of fortune-telling. He was sentenced to spend two weeks in prison

and an hour in the pillory, after which he was banished from London.

Despite his obviously good intentions, the fortune-teller William Byg was arrested in 1467. He had been using a crystal ball as a means of locating a den of thieves, and because of this he was ordered to appear in public, bearing a scroll on his head announcing his crime to the world.

When Henry IV was informed that Lincolnshire was a hotbed of magicians, enchanters, soothsayers, sorcerers and necromancers, he sent a letter to the bishop telling him to investigate the charge, empowering him to root out the malefactors and imprison them. Indeed, ecclesiastical courts would later have a great deal to say concerning the prosecution of potential witches.

We know little about the procedures of these early sorcery and witchcraft trials, but what is significant is that they occurred during times of conflict and that they tended to involve well-known people of the period. When the state finally began to legislate against witches and witchcraft, we can see that there was a conscious decision, over a period of time, to ensure that they were criminal trials and therefore the

province of the secular courts and not a religious matter over which the Church had jurisdiction.

From the very beginning of the reign of Elizabeth I in England, every effort was made to put a definitive statutory instrument together, in which severe penalties for conjuring, sorcery, witchcraft and other related crimes could be imposed. Finally, in 1565, the

ABOVE: Elizabeth I. Many men and women perished during her reign due to the influence of John Jewell, the Bishop of Salisbury.

statute was passed, boldly stating that those who:

'Shall use, practise, or exercise any Witchcraft, Enchantment, Charms or Sorcery, whereby any person shall happen to be killed or destroyed, that counsellors or aiders shall suffer pains of death as a felon or felons.'

Many blame John Jewell, an Anglican of Calvinistic persuasion and the Bishop of Salisbury, for his influence at Elizabeth's court. He persuaded her that a great peril faced her people:

'These kind of people within these last few years are marvellously increased with this Your Grace's realm. These eyes have seen most evident and manifest marks of their wickedness. Your Grace's subjects pine away even unto death, their colour fadeth, their flesh rotteth, their speech benumbed, their senses bereft.

Wherefore, your poor subjects most humble petition unto Your Highness is, that laws touching such malefactors may be put in due execution.'

In most countries, similar acts prohibited black magic, described as the conjuring of spirits, necromancy, and enchantment, making potions (philtres), entertaining spirits, divination, witchcraft, sorcery and invocation. These crimes were on a par

with other more discernible forms of crime, such as heresy, coining (forgery), poisoning and treason.

The net was cast even wider than witchcraft, when psychics and mediums also came within the general descriptions of witchcraft, and included those we would nowadays call faith healers. These were similarly labelled as dabblers in witchcraft, particularly if they used charms or spells.

The traditional use of herbal medicines was also targeted, particularly at a time when the practice

Gazers into crystal balls, mediums and those who used medicinal herbs to make potions were also accused of witchcraft.

of medicine as a profession was beginning to get under way, and it is probable that the influence of doctors,

resulting in the practice of herbalism being defined as witchcraft, had more to do with ridding themselves of competition than anything else. Throughout the world, before medicine was established as a science, the herbalist would have been the first port of call for anyone feeling ill, and it is interesting to note that 'alternative medicine', as we know it today, would have been regarded as witchcraft only half a century ago.

Necromancers were another group to be feared, in that they were reputed

to be able to raise the dead for their own diabolical ends. They were believed to be in league with the Devil, who had given them the power to travel vast distances in a short time as well as the ability to change their shape. As far as many people were concerned, however, the necromancer was yet another individual who had sold their soul for earthly rewards.

Gazers into crystal balls or clairvoyants, who at the time were known as soothsayers or wizards, were

OPPOSITE LEFT & ABOVE RIGHT: Goats and cats were commonly believed to be witches' familiars.

OPPOSITE RIGHT: Witches were reputed to fly through the air on besoms or broomsticks.

ABOVE & RIGHT: Old woodcuts of a witch's cat and dog.

believed to enlist the help of evil spirits to produce images in rings, stones and glass.

Finally, there was the witch herself. The following contemporary description of a witch sums up the fear and loathing in which they were held: 'A witch or hag is a woman that has been deluded by the Devil to enter into a pact with him. She is able to shake the air with thunder and lightning, to cause hail and tempest, and to destroy

FAR LEFT: The tools of the trade.

LEFT & ABOVE: Images of the Devil.

crops and uproot trees. She is given a familiar (a creature in the guise of a goat, cat, calf or pig, etc.), that can help her fly vast distances in a short time. She can also use a broom or a pitchfork to fly. She flies to these distant places to meet with the Devil.'

The witch is clearly identified as an agent of the Devil and as such can cause havoc through her control of the weather. The purpose of her bizarre mode of transport is presumably so that she can engage in sinister orgies and rituals with Satan himself.

Given the fact that society in general believed the Devil to be a very real

ABOVE: A witch riding a goat, by Albrecht Dürer (1417–1528).

ABOVE RIGHT: Anne Boleyn.

RIGHT: Hans Holbein's famous portrait of Henry VIII.

OPPOSITE: Changes in the weather and the destruction of crops were blamed on witches.

presence for evil, who could be encountered at any time, the presumption was that he might induce the unwary or unwise to enter into a liaison with him. Whether or not this fear was already present in the unconscious minds of the common people is unknown, but those who felt it their responsibility to protect the realm and its subjects saw little reason to take a cautious approach when dealing with the forces of evil, wheresoever they should be found.

There were also political reasons why supposed witches should be

targeted. In England, for example, during the reign of Elizabeth I, it was believed that witchcraft and sorcery would be used to restore Catholicism to England and put a Catholic back on the throne. There is an odd story regarding Elizabeth I's persecution of witches, in that it seems to have come from earlier rumours concerning her mother, Anne Boleyn.

It was widely believed that Anne was a witch, although the rumour may have been started in a very real attempt to undermine Elizabeth's position, but in any case the allegation was taken seriously, which could not be ignored by the queen's Protestant subjects.

It is possible that the Emperor Charles V's ambassador, Eustace Chapuys, made the first major accusation on behalf of his king. As part of his attempts to prevent Henry VIII from divorcing Catherine of Aragon and marrying Anne Boleyn, Chapuys described Anne as an evil woman, who 'used witchcraft to manipulate and control the king'. The Catholic priest and writer, Nicholas Sander, compounded the issue by claiming that Anne Boleyn had 'a tumour on her neck and a sixth finger on her right hand'.

28

Had this been the case, the existence of a sixth finger would certainly have been considered proof positive that Anne was a witch, being commonly regarded as a good indicator of the fact. But it was almost certainly not the case, for a Venetian ambassador, who had seen Anne in 1532, described her as being of medium height, very swarthy, with black and beautiful eyes. Even Eustace Chapuys had failed to mention either of the deformities, even though he could be described as a very hostile witness.

Sander also claimed that Anne's father had sent her off to France because she had been having sexual relationships with at least two men, her father's butler and his chaplain. Anne had not, at this stage, even reached puberty and was only seven years old. The most bizarre of the claims was that Anne Boleyn was in fact the daughter of Henry VIII and his supposed mistress, Lady Elizabeth Boleyn. In effect, therefore, Sander claimed that Anne had married her own father.

Henry VIII had been desperate for a male heir and the unfortunate Anne failed to produce a boy. She had given birth to a daughter (later Elizabeth I), and had subsequently miscarried and

then prematurely delivered a deformed stillborn child. Henry would not admit he was capable of fathering such a child and claimed that it was the offspring of a lover instead. Witches were supposed to be unable to bear healthy children, and despite the fact that Anne had produced a perfectly healthy daughter, Henry charged his wife with witchcraft and attempting to poison his eldest daughter, Mary, and the Duke of Richmond, his illegitimate son.

The implications of this charge were clear but needed to be substantiated in order to rid the king of Anne. Given the fact that witches were reputed to have numerous lovers, to poison their enemies, inflict impotence on men, and engage in incest and sodomy, her lovers needed to be unmasked. Henry followed up his charges with the claim that he had been temporarily struck with impotence, and with the aid of his ministers, no less than seven men, including Anne's brother, were accused of cavorting with the queen.

The end result was inevitable: Henry Norris, Mark Smeaton, Sir Francis Weston, William Brereton and George Boleyn were executed on 17 May 1536. They had all been found guilty of having sexual relations with the queen

between October 1533 and December 1535. Sir Thomas Wyatt and Sir Richard Page fared rather better and were exonerated and released. Anne Boleyn, of course, was far less fortunate and was beheaded.

We can begin to piece together the motivations for the witch-hunt craze that swept the world in the 16th and 17th centuries. Firstly was the fact that Christianity had not entirely overcome existing pagan beliefs. Secondly were the power struggles of opposing religious groups to influence their rulers. Thirdly, it presented a means of taking revenge, a way of getting rid of one's rivals, and an easy way of pointing the finger at anyone, who in any way, seemed 'different'. The dangers of witchcraft seemed all too real in more insular and superstitious societies: how better to explain a stillborn child, a cow that produces no milk, or a crop that has failed?

OPPOSITE: One of the reasons for witch hunts were linked with pagan beliefs. These figures are pagan goddesses of fertility.

CHAPTER TWO
SPOTTING A WITCH

*B*lends of truth and superstition have created our modern-day stereotype of the witch. She is female, probably an old woman with an ugly and disfigured face, often spotted with hairy moles. She traditionally wears a pointed hat on her head, is habitually garbed in black, clutches a broomstick, ready to take to the skies, and is accompanied by a sinister black cat.

It is doubtful whether any witch ever looked like this, and it is rather more likely that she was a sad and lonely elderly women or a woman not prepared to hold her tongue, with the result that she was constantly at odds with her neighbours.

But it was not a case of identifying a witch simply from the way she looked. It had more to do with finding someone on whom to lay the blame, whenever a mishap or tragedy occurred. No doubt gossip, jealousy and prejudice, or the fact that a woman was simply a thorn in her neighbour's side, would all have come into the equation. The next step was to point the finger

and find a reason to denounce the woman as a witch, bringing her to the attention of either the witch-hunters or, in extreme circumstances, the assizes.

Simple examples of odd behaviour, used as reasons to denounce someone as a witch, could include talking to oneself or being seen to utter something under one's breath, which would be construed as laying a curse. Even talking to a pet animal was taken

to indicate she was a witch communicating with her familiar.

ABOVE: This woodcut shows three so-called witches, accompanied by their familiars.

OPPOSITE: Many old women were accused of witchcraft, and it was an easy matter to cast them in the role.

Bearing in mind that familiars were considered to be demons, manifested within any animal form, it would inevitably be concluded, provided one looked the part and talked to one's pet, that the creature was the gift of the Devil and that the recipient would have the Devil's marks upon her body.

These marks were believed to be proof positive of a liaison with Satan. Also called witches' marks, they were said to appear on a witch's body after the Devil had bestowed the familiar. Since a Devil's mark could take many mundane forms, such as birthmarks, moles, scars, or even extra nipples, it is not surprising that most individuals should have had one or another. If it was a nipple, then it was believed to produce a milky fluid, or even blood, on which the familiar fed.

Some of the major witch-hunters believed that the Devil's mark only appeared on witches whom the Devil distrusted. Not all witches had familiars, but for those who did, they were intended as the eyes and ears of the Devil. The witch being regarded as untrustworthy, the familiar would then pass on information and observations concerning the witch's behaviour and her adherence to her master's purposes.

As a result, and having been physically examined, unblemished suspects were considered devout and trusted servants of the Devil.

Courts, witch-hunters, and the public in general, had different ways of identifying a witch and establishing her guilt. The judgements of the courts, that condemned witches to death, were based on spurious, confusing and often contradictory evidence. Many of the judges, such as Matthew Hale, ardently believed that witchcraft and pacts with the Devil existed, and evidence was extracted from suspects by numerous and dubious methods of interrogation. A confession made, even while the individual was under extreme duress, was taken as incontravertible proof of guilt.

When the local population took the law into its own hands, the proof that a woman was indeed a witch was based

An engraving from the book, The Lancashire Witches: a Romance of Pendle Forest, *by William Harrison Ainsworth. Alizon Device, accused of witchcraft, is recoiling from an old crone wearing the typical garb of a witch. She is in fact Mother Chattox, who is also accused of being a witch.*

LEFT: An engraving of witches, familiars and demons.

BELOW: Witches feeding a familiar.

While the suspect was under interrogation, she would be placed in a bare cell and watched carefully to see if an animal or insect entered and appoached the suspect. Assuming that such places were invariably vermin-infested, it was inevitable that a cockroach, beetle, rat or mouse would make an appearance. This was immediately taken to be a familiar, on the most spurious of methods, the most popular of these being ducking; this was open to various interpretations that invariably meant death.

A rather more obscure way of judging what was invariably found to be guilt was the use of balancing scales. The suspect would be placed on one side of the scales and an item such as a Bible or weights were placed on the other. If the scales perfectly balanced, then the suspect was presumed not guilty of the accusations made against her. Heavier than the Bible or the weights and there was no doubt that she was a witch.

SPOTTING A WITCH

LEFT: Any animal could be a witch's familiar, and dogs and cats, being the most common and ordinary domestic pets, figured largely in the role.

BELOW: The person accused of witchcraft was often thrown into a bare cell and watched carefully to see if any creature – beetle, rat or mouse – entered the room. When this invariably occurred it was taken for granted that a familiar had come to rescue what was undoubtedly a witch.

sent by the Devil to help the witch make her escape.

It was also believed that witches paid dues to the Devil, although it is never clear how this was done; it is generally assumed that it was the forfeiture of their immortal souls.

Since the pact with the Devil involved a paper contract, this would have been made at the insistence or with the assistance of an existing witch. Back in 1435, *Formicarus* purported to give an example of how these pacts were made. Initally, the candidate had to be chosen and proposed by an existing witch. The new recruit would then be required to go to church on a Sunday morning, before services had begun, and renounce God, the Church and the Bible. Having returned to the coven, the recruit would then drink the blood of a sacrificed child and swear to abide by the coven's rules. The recruit then pledged their soul in return for favours granted to them by the Devil, said to take the form of earthly powers or great wealth.

The pact was sealed when the recruit signed their soul away using their own blood, drawn from their left arm. To avoid the natural propensity of the blood to coagulate, it was warmed over a fire, making it fluid enough to be used as ink; this also signified that a person's intellect was being overcome by passion.

The names given to witches around Europe is most interesting, indicating not only that society was aware of their presence, but also that many of them were regarded as beneficial.

BELOW: New witches were required by the Devil to enter a church and renounce God.

BENANDANTI (Good Walkers)

The Benandanti, an ancient agrarian cult of white witches, originating in the Friuli of Italy, fought a nightly battle to

protect livestock and crops from evil witches (*malandanti*), believing that infants born with a caul (foetal membrane) over parts of their faces had the ability to identify such malefactors. The Benandanti collected these cauls and wore them around their necks as amulets to assist them in their work. Many of them were able to enter into coma-like states, when they would go into battle, riding cats, goats and horses, to drive off the evil walkers. The Benandanti used fennel stalks to repel the witches, who retaliated with the sorghum stalks from which their brooms were made.

The Benandanti became the target of the Inquisition in around 1640, and they admitted their heresy, even though they believed their shamanistic role was essentially good. The result of their clash with the Inquisition meant that their reputation as protectors of the local people was forever discredited.

BRAG (Female Shape-Changer)
The use of this word to describe a witch appears to have come from the original

LUCIFER *The fallen angel*

FAR LEFT: The Archangel Michael slaying Lucifer (Satan), the Fallen Angel. From the Abbaye of St.-Michel de Frigolet, Provence, France.

BELOW: An engraving of Lucifer, who was the Bearer of Light before his fall from grace.

Celtic usage of the word, *Breugache*, which describes a deceitful woman, who disguises herself by changing herself into another form. It is more usually another term for a satyr, so to apply it to a witch was not entirely accurate.

EYE-BITER
It was common practice throughout the witch-hunting period to blame witches or suspected witches for inflicting all manner of ills on humankind, its livestock and crops. The term eye-biter came into use in Ireland during the reign of Queen Elizabeth I, when witches were blamed for an epidemic afflicting cattle. The virus, or what was regarded as an evil spell, caused the cattle to become blind. The witches were given the sobriquet not only because they had blinded the cattle, but also because they had gazed malevolently at the creatures (given them the evil eye).

HAG

The word remains closely associated with stereotypical images of witches as old and ugly women, who have given themselves to the Devil and evil workings. The word has also been used in relation to supernatural beings – often giants – and appears to have some connection with very ancient, elemental nature deities.

LAMIA

Lamia, in Greek mythology, like her daughter Scylla, was but one of the monstrous supernatural demons sent to terrify children and the naive. The Lamia had the head and torso of a woman although the lower half of her body was serpent-like. Lamia comes from the Greek word for gullet, and she was reputed to have a cannibalistic appetite for children that could also be interpreted as an unnaturally erotic

ABOVE RIGHT & RIGHT: These amulets are used to defend a person from the evil eye.

FAR RIGHT ABOVE: The witch as an old hag dates back hundreds of years and is an enduring image to this day, seen in the costumes children wear at Halloween.

appetite for men. It is said that grief turned Lamia into a monster after the goddess Hera killed all her children, leaving only Scylla behind. Lamia was able to take her eyes out and put them back in, which was an attribute of sibyls with the gift of second sight.

LILITH

According to the Talmud, Lilith was the first wife of Adam, who was

supplanted by Eve. She is the female demon of Jewish folklore and is reputed to kill newborn infants. In Mesopotamia she was a storm demon, associated with pestilence and death.

MALEFICA (Demon-Taught Witch) This was a very general term for a witch, based on the assumption that most of them had only evil acts in mind. It was believed that the main aim of a *malefica*, who had obviously been well-instructed by a demon, was to inflict nothing but pain and terror on her victims.

LEFT: Diana the Huntress, *painted c.1550 by an unknown artist. The leader of the Wild Hunt of the Oskorei was always a woman, known to Latin writers as Diana.*

OPPOSITE LEFT: Remains of a castle in the Languedoc region of the Pyrénées. This mountainous region was inhabited by the Poudoués or Poudouéros.

OPPOSITE RIGHT: Sir Francis Drake, by Marcus Gheeraerts the Younger. It is said that the Devil sent sea witches to brew up the storm that allowed Drake to defeat the Spanish Armada in 1588.

OSKOREI (The Wild Hunt)

The Oskorei are an integral part of Norse folklore, although the word is not generally used to describe witches. The myth of the Wild Hunt occurs in many places, and was often mentioned in the witch trials of the Middle Ages. The name of the leader of the Oskorei varies from place to place and it is curiously always a woman, known as the 'bright one', which explains why Latin writers referred to her as Diana the Huntress. On stormy nights, the wild band of the Oskorei, accompanied by their barking hounds, rode the skies looking for the bodies of the recently dead. Having discovered an unclaimed soul, they would descend from the skies and scoop it up, leaving a flaming torch where the body had lain.

POUDOUÉS OR POUDOUÉROS

In a age when sanitation would not have been a primary concern, it seems that witches, warlocks and heretics in the Pyrenees could be identified by their odour, the name given to them having been derived from a word meaning putrescent.

SEA WITCH (Ghost of a Dead Witch)

According to some accounts it was not his own prowess that allowed Sir Francis Drake to become one of the most celebrated mariners in history. At some point prior to his finest hour in 1588, he sold his soul to the Devil in return for victory over the Spanish

SPOTTING A WITCH

Armada. Sea witches accordingly appeared, sent by the Devil, and created a storm that scattered the Spanish fleet, allowing Drake to win a famous victory for England.

Sea witches are said to be the ghosts of dead witches, who inhabit coastal waters, their main purpose being to lure mariners to their deaths.

At Devonport, on the south coast of England, there is a place called Devil's Point, which is reputedly the place where the battle took place, and where the sea witches who helped Drake still lie in wait for unwary victims.

STREGA

A *strix* (plural *striges*) was a fabulous creature in ancient Rome, usually described as a nocturnal bird of ill-omen, that rather like a vampire fed upon human flesh and blood. The word is Greek in origin and means 'owl', by which the largest species of owl is classified today.

The legend of the *strix* survived into the Middle Ages, and also into the name for the Italian witch, *strega*, described as a blood-sucking female active at night, and with the ability to turn themselves into screech owls.

The Christian Church viewed these creatures not only as witches but also as demons and the servants of the Devil. Gradually the term spread to describe any witch practising sorcery, particularly those who were able to fly. Besides sucking the blood of children, *strege* also cast their spells on men, causing their genitals to waste away.

VENEFICA (Adept at Poisoning)

In 1555 Johann Trithemius wrote *Antipalus Maleficorum* in which a clear distinction was made between a true witch, who was in league with the Devil, and a *venefica*, a maker of potions, who has come to mean a female poisoner. As abbot of a Benedictine monastery, Trithemius recognized the fact that many herbalists were capable of brewing up concoctions that were quite as deadly to the Christian flock as the machinations of any witch.

Venefica derives from *veneficium*, an ecclesiastical term that distinguishes between those who made simple herbal love potions and those who used diabolical means to enchant. This was in direct contradiction to the belief that poisoners had supernatural powers by which they could either kill or cure.

WARLOCK (A Traitor or Deceiver)

Although the word warlock is closely associated with the practice of witchcraft and sorcery, it did not become a common term associated with magic until the 14th century. As far as

ABOVE LEFT: The Witch's Daughter, by Frederick S. Church. Many witches are able to assume animal forms, such as the strega, *who turns herself into a screech owl to pursue her prey.*

OPPOSITE: The means of making poisons. The venefica, *once a herbalist, is now defined as a female poisoner.*

the Old English meaning is concerned, it can mean a traitor, a deceiver, an oath-breaker, a male witch, or the Devil himself.

FLYING WITCHES

Many of the stories of witches flying through the air seem to derive from the mythology surrounding the Roman goddess Diana, whose Wild Hunt rode the night skies looking for the unwary to destroy. It would seem that such tales of Diana and her Oskorei (see page 39) may have become synchretized with the later *strega*, the flying witch of Italy.

The method of going to Sabbats and Esbats differed according to the distance that needed to be traversed. In most cases, witches travelled on foot, but more magical methods were used if the distance was too great to walk. This was achieved by using flying ointment, also known as green ointment, magic salve,

LEFT: An illustration from The Lancashire Witches, *by William Harrison Ainsworth. The idea of flying witches may have come from the mythology of the Roman goddess Diana.*

OPPOSITE: Witches were said to be able to turn themselves into carrion crows.

and lycanthropic (pertaining to werewolves) ointment, which was applied to the skin and contained alkaloids such as hemlock, wolfbane, belladonna and henbane and had an hallucinogenic effect. Connected with this was the belief, prevalent among certain European cultures, that witches could transform themselves into werewolves, which in turn sprang from the belief that vampires were the offspring born from couplings between werewolves and witches.

CHANGING SHAPE

What is particularly interesting about contemporary views on changing shape is that, while people believe that witches could fly, they do not believe they could change themselves into something else. As early as the 12th and 13th centuries in Britain, the superstition existed that witches often took the form of animals, and that if they happened to be injured while in that form, they retained evidence of the injury when they returned to their normal human shape. Certain birds were particularly associated with witches, such as crows, jackdaws, magpies and ravens, which is significant in that they all consume carrion. They are also large and black

45

SPOTTING A WITCH

BELOW: The Celts believed that witches could turn themselves into hares.

FAR RIGHT: It was thought that the sexual union of a witch and a werewolf created a vampire.

and make sounds that could easily be mistaken for the human voice.

Certainly in Celtic Scotland, Wales and Ireland, witches were believed to be able to transform themselves into hares, when they would drain the milk from the udders of their neighbours' cows. There were also reports of witches in

Yorkshire, who could turn themselves into hedgehogs and ferrets.

THE EVIL EYE

Prior to the Christian era, people readily accepted that a malevolent force for evil was at work, acting at variance with the force for good. By the time Christianity had become the dominant religion in Europe, it was to the Devil and his agents that the people looked, and witches were prime examples of such demonic agents.

The concept of casting an 'evil eye' is still one that is commonly feared to

this day. Witches able to bewitch or fascinate with a glance were known as *fascinatrix* (bewitchers), and the superstitious believed they could also induce a fatal disease, merely by gazing on their victims.

The casting of an evil eye is synonymous with casting a spell, but without the rituals associated with the latter. It was known as *maleficium*, and could be described as the witch's own ability to do harm. In certain places it was believed that if one suspected one

ABOVE: Yorkshire witches had the power to change themselves into ferrets.

RIGHT: Witches were blamed for creating the weather conditions responsible for damaging crops.

had been inflicted with the evil eye, to spit on the floor would break the spell.

New-born infants in contemporary Greece are still given amulets in the form of eyes to protect them from harm, and the charms are pinned to the baby's clothes during the first few years of its life. It is useless to buy such a charm for oneself, because its ability to protect only works if it is a gift.

Crops damaged by frost or rotted by damp would also be attributed to the *maleficium* of local witches, and they would be similarly blamed for creating the weather conditions that caused these misfortunes to occur. Besides the casting of the evil eye, it was also believed that, by her evil incantations and the conjuring up of demons, witches could cause stillbirths, miscarriages and deformed children to be born.

The modern stereotype of the witch – with pointed hat, cat, broom and

THIS PAGE & OPPOSITE: To many, black cats, broomsticks and cauldrons were part of the paraphernalia used by witches.

cauldron – does not begin to explain the confused and contradictory superstitions and traditions that were current during the height of the witch-hunts. These so-called witches, regardless of their innocence or naïvety, were objects of the greatest fear and loathing, that was whipped up by Church and state. It was accepted that witches had no power themselves and that whatever they possessed came from the Devil. It was this supposed relationship that set them apart from the rest of humanity and which ultimately spelled their doom.

CHAPTER THREE

WITCHES' TOOLS, FAMILIARS & SPELLS

*M*any items a witch used were natural products, approved by the Devil or demons with whom she had made a pact. Objects such as brooms, cauldrons, pins, and hats had an occult meaning, along with magic brews, herbs, liquids, diagrams, circles and pentacles.

TOOLS

AIGUILLETTE A loop of knotted thread, also known as a ligature, was used to create impotence in a man, barrenness in a woman. When a priest was blessing a man's marriage, a witch would tie a knot in the thread and throw a coin on the ground as a gift to the Devil. If it disappeared, the man would keep the curse until Judgement Day and the newly-married couple would be faced with a sterile marriage, in which adultery and unhappiness predominated.

A witch's box, in which the tools of her evil trade were kept.

ATHAME The witch's magical knife was made of a magnetic metal and had a double-edged blade. It often had a black hilt and was covered in magic symbols. As a masculine symbol it was often used in conjunction with a feminine symbol, such as a cup, to mix concoctions, also to scratch magic circles into the earth.

ABOVE: The pentacle is a magical device. When it is placed within the triangle of evocation it is used to call up spirits.

RIGHT: An athame or athamé is a knife used in magic rituals.

BODY PARTS Witches who had been delivered of children themselves would have had access to afterbirths, cauls and umbilical cords, while miscarriages or stillborn babies were another source of body parts.

Witches used the fat from children's bodies to make flying ointment, an aid to flying, and would routinely harvest the body parts of criminals who had been left to rot on the gibbet. Penises, toenails and fingernails were particularly useful in magic ritual.

BROOMSTICKS These certainly figured in pagan rituals dating from the time of the Greeks. It was a symbol of Hecate, the Triple Goddess, whose priestess-midwife, after the birth of a child, swept the threshold of a house to rid it of evil spirits. In the Middle Ages a woman propped her broom against the door or pushed it up the chimney to indicate she was not at home.

The witch's broomstick or besom, possibly a phallic symbol, was a gift

from the Devil, and witches used an hallucinogen before mounting them and taking to the air. They also used a magic flying ointment, which they made from toxic alkaloids, to help them get to the Sabbats and Esbats and to fly far out to sea, where they would conjure up storms.

CAULDRONS The witch made her poisons, ointments and philtres in a vessel such as this, but it was not always a conventional pot made of iron. Lady Alice Kyteler, the 14th-century Irish witch, used the skull of an executed criminal, while the Greek sorceress, Medea, used her magic

OPPOSITE: A modern version of a Book of Spells.

RIGHT: A witch's cauldron.

cauldron to help Jason in his task of finding the Golden Fleece.

Toads, bats, snakes, fat from a child and blood from animals, were only some of the things used in a witch's cauldron.

DOLLS These were simple effigies of intended victims, originally used for love spells but preferred by witches to commit acts of long-distance murder. Nail clippings, hair or sweat, blood or semen from the prospective victim, were fashioned into the design so that the spell would find the correct victim. Fashioned from twisted and plaited straw, tied bundles of small sticks, or a lump of clay, the doll did not have to resemble the victim.

ELF ARROWS Stone-age arrowheads were fashioned from flint and were once used by hunter-gatherers. Witches were accused of using them to kill people, more often cattle, and having been touched by one of these arrows cattle would waste away and die.

GRIMOIRES From the French *grammaire* (grammar), these were books of magic spells and incantations owned by wizards and sorcerers. They were written in an arcane language, and gave instructions on how spirits and demons could be summoned up. They had to be a gift, because the exchange of money cancelled out the effectiveness of the spells. Grimoires

OPPOSITE LEFT: Dolls like this were rough effigies of the witch's victim.

OPPOSITE RIGHT: Discarded stone-age arrowheads were used by witches to cause cattle to waste away and die.

LEFT: Blood, human fat, horse dung and spices were used to make candles, then put into holders made from human hands.

were large books, bound in human or black animal skin, the contents having been hand-written onto parchment in red ink.

HANDS OF GLORY These were candle-holders, fashioned from the right hands of criminals, preferably ones who had been hanged at a place where two roads crossed. Using an earthenware pot, the witch would marinate the hand in herbs and spices for around two weeks before letting it dry in the sunlight. If it was rainy it was put into a slow oven with a mixture of fern and vervain to dry it out. This provided a holder for a candle made out of blood and fat rendered from the body of the dead man, mixed with horse dung, sesame seeds and wax. The wick of the candle was fashioned from

the hanged man's hair. Once lit, a spell could then be cast on anyone in the vicinity, placing them fully under the witch's control.

NEEDLES Aside from inflicting pain on a victim from afar when stabbed into effigies, needles could also be used to injure or kill animals. This had to be done with a needle that had been used to sew up a shroud, and the witch would stick the needle into the ground over which her victim would inevitably pass. When the animal walked over the spot, it would be struck lame or begin a slow decline towards death.

PENTACLES AND PENTAGRAMS
A pentacle is an upright five-pointed star, set within a circle, while a pentagram is a pentacle reversed; they are the most powerful symbols within the world of occultism. They appear in old grimoires, such as the Key of Solomon, where they are said to bestow a knowledge of the future, give power over nature and the spirit world, and to perform miracles.

Alternatively, pentacle may possibly symbolize one of the following: either God and the four elements of nature; the five senses of man; or an

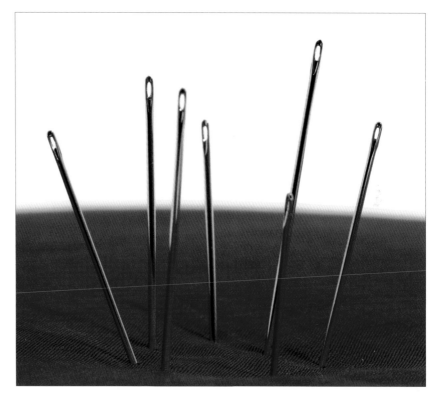

outstretched man with his head, arms and legs at each point and his genitals in the centre, rather like Leonardo's depiction of Vitruvian Man.

In witchcraft, pentacles were drawn with the uppermost point representing Hecate, the Triple Goddess, who represents maiden, mother and crone, and as Mistress of the Night symbolizes the three phases of the moon. Witches and occultists used

these devices to conjure up spirits or as protections against more malevolent demons.

OPPOSITE: This pentacle is worn as a protective amulet. In magic, however, it can be used for both good and evil purposes.

ABOVE: Needles were used by witches, plunged into effigies, to injure or kill victims from afar.

OPPOSITE: A somewhat older pentacle, used to protect the doorway to a building.

RIGHT: Besides being used for the more legitimate handling of hay, witches also used pitchforks as well as broomsticks on which to fly.

BELOW: Pins have long been connected with superstitions and magic practices.

PINS According to superstition, one should always pick up pins in case a witch finds them and uses them for magic purposes. Bent pins were put into potions both to cast spells and to break the spells of other witches. Sticking pins into fruit at midnight, while uttering a magic incantation, was believed to confer prosperity.

PITCHFORKS Used as an alternative mode of transport by witches, pitchforks were more practical than broomsticks as useful items could be attached to the prongs, such as cauldrons. Witches were also reputed to attach cloths to the prongs as sails, that helped their passage through the air.

QUIRIN A quirin (quirus) was a stone found in birds' nests, particularly those of lapwings. Said to have the power of discovering the truth, they were placed beneath a person's pillow at night, compelling them to confess their wrongdoings the following morning.

SPECULA

Specula are witches' balls, used for divination or seeing into the future. Glass or crystal balls are not the only kind of specula, and mirrors and polished stones are also used. Witches believed that by staring into their depths they could see not only far into the future, but see places never visited before and discover the answers to imponderable questions.

Witches' balls, around 7in (18cm) in diameter and made of blue or green glass, were often found in fishing villages, used by fishermen to keep their nets afloat.

Mirrors were used by witches when preparing love spells and charms. The witch would write the name of the person and the intended beloved on the back of a scrying mirror before finding two mating dogs and capturing their reflection in the mirror. The mirror would then be covered and taken to the person to be enchanted, who on gazing into the mirror, would be struck with

unbridled lust for the person to whom they had been magically bound.

A speculum had no power unless it had been exposed to the light of a full moon and protected from direct sunlight. It was only used at night, and was not affected by candlelight.

SPINNING-WHEELS AND THREAD

Although witches did not use spinning-

wheels or spinning as part of their magical activities, a number of spindles from spinning-wheels have been

ABOVE: Often used to see into the future, a witch's ball can also be hung in a window to prevent evil from entering a house.

RIGHT: Witches also used mirrors for casting love spells.

warm it by a fire, then rub it onto the back of her own animal. This had the dual effect of improving the milk yield of the witch's animal, while reducing that of her neighbour's.

URINE At the Sabbat, witches anointed new initiates with urine, in mockery of Christian baptism, and routinely used urine as a perversion of Holy Water.

FAMILIARS Many witches had familiars, which were given to them by the Devil, either to help them in their craft or to spy on those whom the Devil mistrusted. The usual familiars were cats and dogs, although toads, rats and hares were also common. A familiar, being a spirit, could transform itself into any guise. The witch nurtured it either by mixing her own blood with the familiar's food, or by suckling the familiar, as she would a child, by means of a hidden nipple, with blood mixed with milk.

The witch's ability to transform herself into a cat was limited to nine occasions, hence the notion that a cat had nine lives. Witches would often renew their pact with the Devil by gathering in the presence of a black cat, when they would lift the cat's tail, and kiss the anal area.

unearthed by archeologists from the ancient graves of witches.

Apart from thread in the form of an aiguillette or ligature (page 52), a thread was also used to induce a cow, goat or sheep to produce less milk. A witch would stretch a thread across the path habitually taken by a neighbour's animal. After the beast had broken the thread the witch would take it and

OPPOSITE: Spinning-wheels and threads have associations with witchcraft.

BELOW: Urine was used at Sabbats for initiating new members into a coven.

RIGHT: Dogs and wolves, among many other creatures, could be witches' familiars.

Bees, flies, mice and spiders could also be familiars and suspected witches were often accused of making fetishes and idols from beeswax, in the form of demons and the Devil, or of a person or animal they intended to bewitch.

A witch could obtain a familiar when another living witch gave the creature up to her voluntarily, or it could be inherited from a dead witch or during a magical ceremony of some description. It was commonly thought that witches had intercourse with chickens and that some, after mating with cockerels, continued to produce eggs each day.

SPELLS

BOOK OF SHADOWS This was a witch's bible of witchcraft, where all the chants, spells, dances, incantations, herbal lore, rituals and beliefs needed to carry out her craft could be found. Covens usually had a single copy, kept by the High Priest or Priestess.

CAULDRON LORE The cauldron symbolizes the womb of the Great Goddess and therefore the feminine principle. It represents germination, transformation and transmutation. It is bound to the belief that everything is born from the cauldron and returns to it. Witches believed the Goddess gave them inspiration, knowledge and wisdom every time they used it.

CONES OF POWER This was a technique whereby psychic energy or

power could be created. The witches joined hands within a magic circle, which they danced around, chanting while visualizing their purpose. The cone's base was the circle and it extended above the witches into infinity.

LEFT: Even spiders were occasionally witches' familiars.

ABOVE: Incantation: The Lancashire Witches, *by William Harrison Ainsworth.*

OPPOSITE: A cauldron bearing the symbol of Hecate, the Triple Goddess.

instructions to Hitler to persuade him not to invade the British Isles. Witches also used cones to help Sir Francis Drake defeat the Spanish Armada in 1588 and in the latter half of the 18th century against Napoleon Bonaparte.

CROSSROADS Signifying a joining of paths and the union of opposites. The crossroads was a powerful symbol that existed in ancient Greece. The goddess Hecate was the guardian of the crossroads, having the power to see in several directions at once.

CURSES These are magic spells intended to bring misfortune to others. Witches laid curses on people, usually as a way of seeking revenge. Not all curses took immediate effect, neither did their strength diminish with the death of the intended victim.

The most common way of laying a curse was to create a doll or effigy, which in most cases resembled the intended victim, and once harm had been done to the effigy the victim would be similarly harmed. If the effigy was subsequently destroyed, such as by being cast into a fire, then the victim would die. An alternative was to prick the effigies with thorns, pins or knives.

The Egyptians were probably experts at laying curses; a wax figure of a demon, known as Apep, would be created, and the name of the victim would be written on it. The effigy would then be wrapped in papyrus and thrown into a fire. While it was burning it would be kicked with the left foot four times, and once the effigy had been reduced to ashes it would be mixed with excrement and thrown into another fire.

Death-bed curses were the most powerful. Witches believed that the best time to lay a curse was during the waning of the moon.

DRAWING DOWN THE MOON
To bring all present closer to the deity, the High Priestess of a coven would enter into a dream-like state, when she would adopt the persona of the Goddess. The Goddess was symbolized by the moon and with the assistance of the High Priest, the moon would be drawn into the High Priestess's body.

FAR LEFT: Cones of power were supposedly used to defeat Napoleon.

RIGHT: Once it had been drawn down, the moon, symbolizing the Great Goddess, brought all present closer to the deity.

Perhaps the most famous application of the cone of power in Britain was the one created on Lammas Day, 1 August 1940, in the New Forest in England to project telepathic

EAST The east is connected with the rising of the sun and moon, which is the direction of enlightenment. It is linked with the eagle, the power of the mind and knowledge. Many witches oriented their altars towards the east.

ESBATS These were regular meetings of witches' covens that always ended in the sharing of food and drink. Esbats were held on nights when the moon was full (13 times a year), while others met to celebrate the new moon or held Esbats simply as weekly meetings. Esbats took place either out of doors or in one of the witch's homes. It was believed that witches attended these meetings naked, but it is more likely that they wore robes or loose clothing.

EVIL EYE Casting an evil eye can occur either involuntarily, when there is no evil intent, or deliberately.

LEFT: The east is connected with the rising of the sun and moon.

OPPOSITE PAGE: Belief in the evil eye is more prevalent in Latin countries, where people are brown-eyed, and this is the reason why such protective devices take the form of blue eyes.

The deliberate or malevolent use of the evil eye is also known as overlooking, when misfortunes such as illness, poverty, injury, loss of love, or even death can be suffered by the victim. Witches in the Middle Ages were reputed to give the evil eye to just about anyone who annoyed them.

FASCINATION This was a way of bewitching a victim through a process resembling hypnosis, by which the subject would become so transfixed that they quickly surrendered to the witch's will.

FERMENTATION To sow dried seeds into the earth symbolized death and a

descent to the underworld. The process of new life coming from something that appeared dead was a reflection of the Goddess's meeting with the Lord of the Underworld. When the seed began to sprout, the Goddess was seen to have returned and the plant itself was considered a god, known as the Child of Promise. The Goddess represented the spirit of the plant and the Child of Promise was its physical presence, which would eventually become the

ABOVE: The seeds of autumn provide next year's crop, echoed in Persephone's return from Hades each spring.

OPPOSITE: The feminine symbol of the chalice was used in the Great Rite.

Horned God or Harvest Lord, whose interaction with the Goddess produced the seed from which new life would emerge next spring.

FERTILITY Witches could have a positive or a negative effect on the fertility of human beings, livestock and crops. Many midwives, practising in the 16th century, were accused of being witches on the grounds that they could cause or prevent pregnancies. It was also believed that they could either make a birth easy and relatively painless or difficult, painful and protracted. It was also said that they could transfer the pain of labour from a woman to her husband or an animal.

FLYING Flight was associated with the ancient belief that witches could transform themselves into birds, particularly ravens or owls, although it was not until the Middle Ages that this came to be associated with the Devil. The belief that witches used other objects to help them fly, such as broomsticks or demons in the form of animals, developed over the centuries.

GREAT RITE Symbolizing the union between men and women and the God

LEFT: Gold or silver rings were exchanged during the Handfasting ritual.

OPPOSITE: The forces of darkness were at their most powerful on the shortest day of the year.

a coven, and could be described as wise women, who understood the power of natural remedies and used them for the benefit of the local community. Their practices differed greatly from those of other witches.

INITIATION Initiation into the craft symbolized the death of the candidate and their rebirth as a witch. This was a symbolic act by which they were given or could develop their magical powers, and was seen as a spiritual transformation. To achieve this, witches had to come to a meeting, presided over by the Devil, which was held in a remote place at night. Here they would renounce Christ and embrace the Devil as their new god.

LIBATION This simple act was performed by witches to honour their deity. A cup or chalice would be filled with wine and each in turn would pour a small amount onto the ground in

and Goddess, the Great Rite required complete union, physically, mentally and spiritually, through sexual intercourse. The rite, usually performed by the High Priest and High Priestess, took place within a magic circle at a Sabbat or other meeting of the coven. The union did not have to involve actual physical congress, but when it did the onlookers would turn their backs or leave the couple until they had finished. When the act was merely symbolic, the High Priest would put his athame or ritual knife, which

represented a phallus, into a cup or chalice representing the female womb.

HANDFASTING The witch's equivalent of marriage, this ritual bound a couple together, not necessarily for life but for as long as they continued to love one another. Gold or silver rings were exchanged and many couples jumped onto a broomstick for good luck. Divorce was known as Handparting.

HEDGE WITCHES These were solitary witches who did not belong to

front of her, while gazing at the moon. Alternatively, they would scatter food towards the moon, kissing their left hands and raising them in the air.

LIGHT AND DARKNESS Dualism exists in all things, often in opposition, such as male and female, right and wrong, good and evil, light and darkness. Light and darkness, summer and winter are features of the Wheel of the Year, which describes how the Goddess ages and rejuvenates endlessly with the seasons, her different aspects having been both lover and mother of the Horned God.

The forces of darkness were at their most powerful on the shortest day of the year, but as light and darkness were different faces of the same coin, the ultimate wisdom could be achieved through a balance of the two.

MAGIC WORDS The most powerful of these were used to raise the Devil, or to conjure up or summon a familiar. Witches used magical incantations to allow them to cross water without getting wet and to turn themselves back into their original form after they had transformed themselves into animal shapes.

NECROMANCY Necromancy should not be confused with conjuring up devils or demons for help. Necromancy is raising the spirits of the dead, in the belief that they are no longer limited by their physical bodies or confined to the earthly plane. Witches believed these spirits now roamed freely, both in the past and the future, and could be used to find missing items, treasure, or the cause of a person's ultimate death.

NORTH This is the most powerful orientation, being associated with winter, the colours black and brown, the human body, and the earth. The north also represented an inability to see clearly in that direction and the North Star was considered to be the centre of the universe, being the living place of gods. It symbolized the power to listen, keep secrets, and know when to remain silent.

RAINMAKING A useful trick both for ruining crops and encouraging them, the interference with nature by witches was recognized as early as 1488 by Pope Innocent VIII. Forty years later, Pope Adrian VI denounced witches 'as a Sect deviating from the Catholic Faith, denying their Baptism, and showing

Contempt of the Ecclesiastical Sacraments, treading Crosses under their Feet, and, taking the Devil for their Lord, destroyed the Fruits of the Earth by their Enchantments, Sorceries, and Superstitions'.

SABBATS At Sabbats, witches were reputed to worship and mate with the Devil and eat forbidden foods, such as

OPPOSITE: A representation of the Sun or Horned God.

BELOW: The North Star was considered by witches to be the centre of the universe.

the flesh of children. The term Sabbat or Sabbath, is derived from the Hebrew, 'to rest'. Sabbats took place on particularly significant days of the year

and many coincided with Christian feasts and holy days.

At a time when the Goddess was preparing to give birth to the Sun or the Horned God, Oimelc centred around the lighting of fires in February. Coinciding with the holy day of Brigid (St. Brigid), the Goddess of fire, healing and fertility. this was later superseded by the Virgin Mary's feast of Candlemas.

The Spring Equinox (March 21) was a solar festival, where male and female were in equilibrium in the birth of the Sun God and the coming of summer.

Beltane (April 20), one of the original Celtic solar festivals, celebrated birth and fertility and the union of the Goddess with the Sun God.

The Summer Solstice (June 21) was the time when herbs were collected at midnight to protect against witchcraft.

Lamas (July 31) was an auspicious time to marry and consummate a union, so that a child's birth would

LEFT: Witches were thought capable of controlling the weather for good or bad, by conjuring up storms and causing rain to fall.

OPPOSITE: The skull signifies renewal or rebirth.

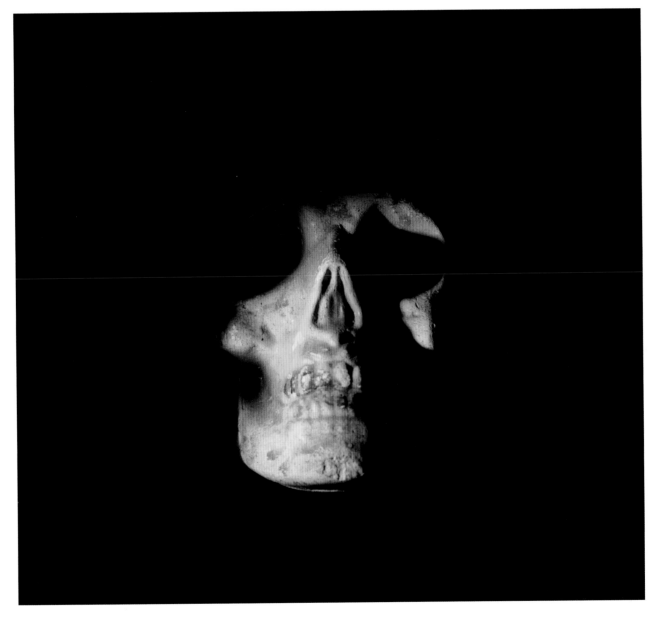

coincide with the Beltane celebration the following year. Its original name having been Lughnasadh, in honour of the Celtic Irish God Lugh, the name Lamas derives from an old Saxon fruit and grain festival, originally initiated by the Church to celebrate the ripening of crops and the time when tenant farmers paid their dues to their landlords in the form of grain.

The Autumn Equinox (September 21), a day when the balance of male and female power was also equal, was the time of the second harvest.

Samhain (October 31) or Halloween (the eve of All Saints Day) – was a time when spirits were wandered abroad. It also celebrated the end of summer, when Druids imprisoned their victims in wicker cages before sacrificing them on huge bonfires.

The Winter Solstice (December 21), the longest night of the year, was when the Goddess awoke to discover she was pregnant with the Sun or Horned God, who was also her lover.

SKULLS These signify renewal through transformation and represent a person's inner nature. In initiation ceremonies, they symbolize the death of the initiate and their re-birth into the new religion.

SOUTH This symbolizes fire, energy and spirit and was closely associated with summer and the middle of the day.

SPELLS These had the power to create or change a course of events. While visualizing her intention, the witch would perform a set procedure or make

OPPOSITE: The Christian Harvest Festival is a remnant of pagan traditions.

BELOW & PAGES 82–83: Today Halloween is seen as a time for harmless fun, even though it had more sinister connotations in the past.

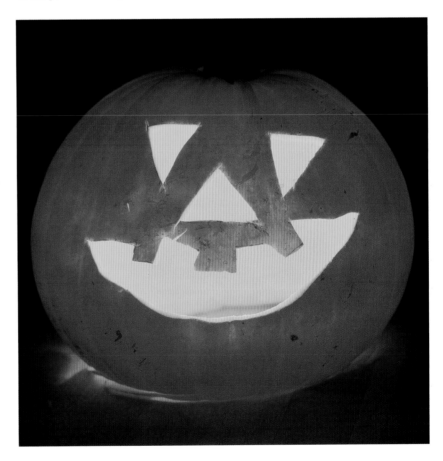

OPPOSITE: *The southerly direction is associated with summer or midday.*

LEFT: *The magic wand has long been seen as a necessity for casting spells. This wand was made by a modern white witch.*

Spells took the form of precisely-worded incantations, but it was first necessary to visualize what the outcome (the cone of power) was to be. Then the intention would be stated and the assistance of the deity would be sought before the request was projected forth. Spells were chanted and movements were performed, perhaps by candlelight, with effigies or an item taken from the intended victim's body in close proximity. Words that rhymed were used in incantations to increase their power.

SPITTLE Witches often spat when creating evil spells or curses, particularly when reciting them for the first time, while others spat on stones, which they rubbed as they made their incantations. Others tied three knots in cloth and spat while reciting the name of the victim and praying to the Devil. Many witches believed that if they

gestures or movements, such as shutting her eyes or clasping her hands, to project her will, with the aid of spirits or the Devil, onto the subject of her spell-making.

Casting positive spells, seen as blessings or enchantments, brought protection, prosperity, longevity, love and healing, while spells intended to be inimicable to a victim, termed curses, hexes or bewitchments, caused such misfortunes as impotence, loss of property or love, illness or, in extreme circumstances, death.

obtained a sample of the victim's saliva it would increase the power of the spell.

To protect themselves during interrogation, and because witch-hunters believed witches incapable of shedding tears, witches often smeared saliva onto their cheeks.

SUMMONERS Being male and clad in black, summoners were often associated with or mistaken for the Devil in human guise. The role of the summoner was to visit each witch to tell them where and when meetings or rituals would be taking place, also to screen prospective initiates.

TRANSFORMATION Witches believed they could change their physical shape by using potions or elixirs. LSD, a modern-day hallucinogen, is derived from the mould, *Claviceps purpurea*, or ergot, that is found in rye, and which was used in the making of Sabbat cakes.

The mushroom *Amanita muscaria* was also capable of producing the desired effect, as was the intoxicant *Bufotenin*, an alkaloid compound secreted by toads, while urine from those who had already taken other hallucinogenic drugs formed the basis of many other potions.

WELLS Regarded as entrances to the underworld and to the realms of the spirits and fairies, wells were also symbolic of the Goddess's womb, and well-water also symbolized a woman's bodily fluids.

A woman's menstrual cycle proved that she could bleed without necessarily being ill, therefore menstrual blood was believed to have magical properties and well-water was accordingly believed to have healing powers.

OPPOSITE & PAGES 88–89: The west was associated with water and the underworld. Water magic was based on causing damage by cold weather or hexing a person that resulted in them freezing to death.

ABOVE: Well-water was believed to have healing powers, in that it symbolized the female bodily fluids.

WEST The portal to the underworld was in the west, also associated with water, emotions and autumn.

WHEEL OF THE YEAR This represented the changing seasons and symbolized birth, death and rebirth, that occurred in a never-ending cycle. Each of the wheels eight spokes corresponded with one of the eight major Sabbats of the year. It is thought either to have been a Greek symbol, dating from c.600 BC, or a Celtic concept.

WITCH'S LADDER A cord or a string of beads helped to focus the attention while making incantations. It needed to comprise 40 beads on a string or 40 knots in a cord to ensure a successful spell, and the magic words had to be repeated 40 times. Witches dedicated a particular cord to the laying of a curse, whose knots, both symbolically and in reality, signified the gradual control they were gaining over their victims. The victim would remain under the spell or curse until the cord was found and the knots untied.

OPPOSITE & RIGHT: A witch's ladder.

PAGES 92–93: The tools of a witch's craft.

CHAPTER FOUR
THE WITCH'S GARDEN

ost green-fingered witches would have had a variety of different plants at their disposal from which to make their concoctions, and some of these were extremely dangerous.

Readers should note that the following descriptions of the ways in which these plants were supposedly used by witches, and for what reasons, are given only out of historical interest, and in no circumstances must be imitated.

ALMOND – *Prunus dulcis*
A witch would occasionally have used

BELOW & PAGES 96–97: A well-stocked herb garden was a necessity for a witch if she was to create magical concoctions.

OPPOSITE: Apples have many applications, and make useful remedies for both internal and external complaints.

this plant, particularly when making flying ointments. Almond oil was often mixed with poppy juice, aconite, cinquefoil, poplar leaves and foxgloves, before being added to a lanoline and beeswax base.

APPLES – *Genus Malus*

Apples have long featured in popular folk remedies to cure rheumatism and remove warts. The Anglo-Saxons used them not only as a magical antidote against venom, or poison, but also as a purifier and cleanser. In Celtic folklore the apple tree has magical and spiritual properties and was reputed to provide the user with special powers or knowledge. It was also used as an aid to foretelling the future.

Because apples can be stored throughout the winter, witches used them frequently in a variety of remedies for stomach, bowel and heart complaints, and for making poultices for application to wounds.

BELLADONNA – *Atropa Belladonna*

Belladonna, more commonly known as deadly nightshade, is a perennial plant producing purple bell-shaped flowers and purplish-black berries. It is one of the most toxic plants in existence, in

LEFT: Belladonna, or deadly nightshade, is a highly poisonous alkaloid with hallucinogenic properties.

OPPOSITE: Common culinary herbs and other plants were also used in spells and potions alongside more exotic ingredients.

that it contains powerful tropane alkaloids, which can cause tachycardia, hallucinations, blurred vision, loss of balance, a feeling of flight, staggering, a sense of suffocation, profound confusion and disorientation. Atropine can be extracted from the deadly nightshade and other plants of the family *Solanaceae*. It is potentially deadly, and can devastatingly affect a person's ability to make judgments. Its other effects include blurred vision, sensitivity to light, a dry mouth and incoherent speech, coupled with anxiety, panic and confusion.

Women in 18th-century Italy used a cosmetic made from belladonna (fair lady) as eye drops, which dilated the pupils. This supposedly added to the beauty and brilliance of their eyes and gave their gaze a seductive intensity. It was also known to cause blindness if used too frequently.

In Europe, particularly during the Middle Ages, belladonna was used by occultists and witches, the latter using it to help them see into the future. They also used it, with other ingredients, to concoct their flying ointments, which supposedly helped them take to the air. In 1324 an investigation into the activities of a particular witch reported that: '...in rifleing the closet of the ladie, they found a pipe of oyntment, wherewith she greased a staffe, upon which she ambled and galloped through thick and thin, when and in what manner she listed.'

A later investigation in the 15th century reported that ' ... the vulgar do believe and the witches confess, that on certain days and nights they anoint a staff and ride on it to the appointed place or anoint themselves under the arms and in other hairy places and sometimes carry charms in their hair', also that '... a man who sometimes be changed into a fish, and flinging out his arms, would swim on the ground, sometimes he would seem to skip up and then dive down again. Another would believe himself turned into a goose, and would eat grass, and beat the ground with his teeth like a goose; now and then sing, and clap his wings'.

CINQUEFOIL – *Genus Potentilla*
Witches, when preparing their flying ointments, also used cinquefoil, which was quoted in Nathaniel Hawthorne's *Young Goodman Brown* as being a constituent of a potion used by self-confessed witches.

CORN – *Zea mays*
According to the *Malleus Maleficarum*, the work of two Dominican monks, Henrich Kramer and Jakob Sprenger, corn (maize) and oats were used by witches to feed stolen penises, and they also rode cornstalks in much the same way as they did their broomsticks. In Ireland, it was believed that the cornstalk turned into a horse once a witch climbed onto it.

ELDER – *Sambucus nigra*
The elder tree is also known as the witch's tree and the death tree. A witch would have regularly used all parts of the tree – the leaves, flowers, berries and the bark. In Irish folklore, witches used elder branches as their broomsticks, while other parts were

It is said that witches used cornstalks in much the same way as they did broomsticks on which to fly.

OPPOSITE: Elderflowers were worn as magic emblems.

RIGHT: Fennel has valuable healing and culinary properties.

used to induce vomiting and perspiration and to summon spirits. Elderflowers were worn as emblems of witchcraft and magic and elder twigs were believed to have the power to undo evil magic.

Much superstition surrounds the use of elder, and the Elder Tree Mother is said to follow and haunt the owners of furniture made from an elder that has been chopped down. Elder branches were hung in doorways, thrown into graves, and scattered in four directions as protections against witchcraft. Wine made from elderberries was used as a medicine or herbal remedy for colds and asthma, also as a rub for the chest and throat.

ERGOT - *Claviceps purpurea*
Ergot is a fungus that lives on rye and other grasses and is pathogenic to its host as well as to humans and other animals that ingest it. It can make the unsuspecting victim salivate and vomit, and cause diarrhoea, physical and

mental depression, tremors, a staggering gait, laboured breathing, abdominal cramps, numbness, and coldness of the extremities. Ergot was commonly used by witches and 'midwives' to induce uterine contractions and for its hallucinatory effects; it may also have been used in witches' flying ointment.

FENNEL – *Foeniculum vulgare*
The Benandanti of the Italian Friuli identified, fought, and killed witches in their dreams, wielding the stalks of the fennel plant in their battle to eradicate them from their community. Fennel is also valuable for its curative properties, also as a culinary herb.

FERN – *Genus Aspleniaceae*
Witches used the seed of these ferns or spleenworts to render people invisible and, as the name suggests, it was believed to cure disorders of the spleen. It was the custom in Wales to gather a bunch of ferns and place it near a horse's ears to keep the Devil away and baffle witches.

Common herbs used both in the kitchen and for medicinal purposes.

LEFT: The foxglove is highly poisonous in the wrong hands, although it is used clinically to treat certain heart conditions.

OPPOSITE: Fairies are said to be particularly fond of the hawthorn and will punish anyone who damages the tree.

FOXGLOVE – *Digitalis purpurea*
The common foxglove is also known as witches' gloves, dead man's bells and bloody fingers, which are only some of is many names. It has soft, hairy leaves and produces flowers in its second year of growth. It is used in magic for protection and to communicate with fairies and woodland spirits. Legend has it that foxes put the blossoms on their feet to deaden their footsteps when approaching their prey.

Due to the presence of digitoxin in foxgloves, the leaves, flowers and seeds of this plant are all poisonous to humans and some animals, and can be fatal if eaten. This same compound, however, is used in medicine to treat heart failure

HAWTHORN – *Crataegus oxyacantha*
The garden hawthorn is known by many names, such as whitethorn, hazel, gazel, halves, quickset, and bread-and-cheese.

The flowers, fertilized by insects, are said to smell of the grave if taken into the house, while people with hawthorns in their gardens were in danger of being accused of witchcraft.

The hawthorn, or may, is associated with Beltane and is supposedly beloved of fairies, which seek revenge if the tree is harmed in any way. The thorn apple, the fruit of the hawthorn, is poisonous and its juice was applied to a mother's nipples to kill an unwanted child. It was also used by witches and wizards to increase their power of second sight.

HAZEL – (SEE WITCH HAZEL)

HEATHER – *Calluna vulgaris*
Heather was reputed to open fairy portals, connecting the mortal world with theirs. *Calluna* is derived from the Greek word for 'to sweep', and the plant was used to make brooms. It was also associated with witches' brooms.

HELLEBORE – *Helleborus niger*
Used by ancient herbalists as well as witches, the hellebore or Christmas rose is very poisonous. Its toxins can affect

OPPOSITE & RIGHT: Heather was reputedly used in witches' brooms.

both animals and human beings alike and its leaves produce a burning sensation if pressed to the lips.

HEMLOCK – *Conium maculatum*
Quoted in Shakespeare's *Macbeth* as a component of the witches' brew, hemlock is an extremely poisonous plant, that can easily be mistaken for common parsley.

To render a male impotent, witches used the juice of the hemlock's tiny white flowers. It was also an ingredient in many of the witches' ointments and was the regular home of a witch's toad, that lived beneath the plant and

BELOW: Hemp is a powerful narcotic, used by witches to summon up demons.

sucked up its poisons. Hemlock was one of the magical plants used by female soothsayers, and it was responsible, in ancient Greece, for killing Socrates.

HEMP – *Cannabis sativa*
Witches used hemp, which has narcotic properties, to call up demonic apparitions and to stupefy their victims.

HENBANE – *Hyoscyamus niger*
Henbane belongs to the family *Solanaceae*, along with plants such as the potato, the tomato, deadly nightshade, the mandrake, and the daturas. The seedpods of the plant contain hundreds of small greyish-brown seeds similar to those of the poppy. All parts of the plant are toxic, but the leaves are particularly poisonous, and even their smell can cause dizziness and stupor in some.

Henbane has a sedative effect on the central nervous system, but if taken in large amounts can cause the mouth to dry, dilation of the pupils, restlessness, hallucinations, and delirium leading to coma and ultimately death. Witches used henbane to raise storms, blight crops, and poison animals, and it is one of the legendary plants used in their flying ointments, whereby they experienced hallucinations and felt as though they were flying. When new witches were initiated into existing covens, they were given a concoction containing henbane to drink, when they would experience a feeling of intoxication, a pressure in the head, a sensation as if someone were forcing their eyelids closed, their sight would become unclear, objects would distort in shape, and visual hallucinations would be induced.

JIMSONWEED – *Datura stramonium*
Part of the *Datura* family of plants, Jimsonweed, related to the deadly nightshade, is very poisonous. The plant has large violet or white trumpet-shaped flowers and unpleasant-smelling foliage.

Its name derived from Jamestown, Virginia where, in the 17th century, British soldiers were accidentally drugged with it while attempting to suppress Bacon's Rebellion. They were deranged for several days and it took 11 days for them to recover. They were unable to remember anything of the incident afterwards.

Witches used Jimsonweed to induce hallucinations, and plants of the *Datura* family were used by Native Americans for ceremonial and spiritual purposes, the effects of which were 'like being in a living dream'.

JUDAS TREE – *Genus Cercis*
Traditionally associated with Judas Iscariot, witches frequently used parts of the tree, and it was unlucky to walk close to one after midnight.

LETTUCE – *Genus Lactuca*
Witches have used the common lettuce since the Middle Ages as an ingredient in their ointments, and the white sap contained in the stalk, also known as lettuce opium, was used in their potions. The lettuce would be picked and the sap extracted from the stalk before being dried, ready to be used by the witch.

MANDRAKE – *Atropa mandragora*
Related to deadly nightshade, the pharmacologically active ingredient in mandrake is atropine, which is an alkaloid and highly narcotic.

Tradition has it that the mandrake's roots have magical powers. It was also reputed to shriek when anyone tried to uproot it, because it had supposedly grown from the seed of a dead person executed for murder. Consequently, to prevent demons rising with the roots, three circles would be drawn around the plant with a double-edged sword, or dogs were used to harvest the plant.

THE WITCH'S GARDEN

LEFT: Lettuce has been used in wiches' potions for centuries.

OPPOSITE: Mistletoe is highly poisonous, and is used by witches for casting spells.

In some parts of Europe, to be caught with mandrake root in one's possession was punishable by death. Witches harvested the mandrake at night, washed it in wine and wrapped it in silk and velvet. They would already have had a supply of sacramental wafers, used in communion services, which had been stolen from a church, and the root was regularly fed with these. The crushed root caused hallucinations, followed by a death-like trance. The root could also cause insanity, and was used in love potions and flying ointments. Witches sold their mandrake potions to individuals who desired to discover the secrets of others, to barren women, and to those seeking superior knowledge and wisdom.

The Greek philosopher, Pythagoras, described the mandrake root as 'an anthropomorph' – having the characteristics of a human being – and the plant has been associated with magic

practices ever since. The French regarded the mandrake as a kind of elf or sprite, and its possession often led to charges of witchcraft. In 1630, three women in Hamburg were executed on evidence of possessing the plant, and in Orléans, in 1603, the wife of a Moor was hanged for harbouring a 'mandrake-fiend', purportedly in the shape of a female monkey. In Wales the plant is known as the black bryony, and its leaves and fruit were referred to as 'charnel food'.

MISTLETOE – *Viscum album*

A common species of mistletoe, this is an evergreen parasite that grows on deciduous trees, such as the oak. It is also known as 'witch's broom', because it was used in the casting of spells. Its use was banned by the early Church, because of its association with the pagan Druids, who believed it had magical powers and was a protection from evil. It was reputed to render its wearer invisible, and many believed it spontaneously regenerated itself, which is how it came to be associated with aphrodisiacs and fertility.

MONKSHOOD – *Aconitum napellus*

Aconite and wolfsbane are but two of

frequently combined monkshood with belladonna, another alkaloid, to make their flying ointments, and also mixed it with water parsnip, cinquefoil and soot to make an ointment that intensified the imagination, allowing them to speak to the dead. The ancient Greeks believed the plant originated from the

the monkshood's many other names. It is highly toxic and its root can easily be mistaken for horseradish. The plant has long been associated with werewolves, either to repel them (related to their use for poisoning wolves), or to induce a lycanthropic condition. Witches

ABOVE: The mandrake is said to shriek when uprooted, and magical rituals had to be performed before it could be harvested.

RIGHT & OPPOSITE: Witches' covens often met beneath a spreading oak tree.

LEFT: Witches used the opium in poppies to make potions. (See page 119.)

RIGHT: Oranges were used by witches in charms and love potions.

told the afflicted man to climb a certain tree, and that he might take which he liked out of a nest in which there were several members. And when he tried to take a large one, the witch said, "You must not take that one," adding, "because it belonged to a parish priest.'"

OLIVE – *Olea europaea*
Thriving only in Mediterranean climates or similar, the olive (page 118) is a symbol of peace and sacred to Athena, who created the first tree by plunging her spear into the ground. Olive leaves were used in crowns to honour victors in the ancient Olympic Games. Witches would not necessarily have used olives or their oil in potions, but they would have used the oil to steep other plants in overnight, or alternatively melted lard.

ORANGE – *Citrus vulgaris*
Witches used oranges in charms and love potions or philtres, which they used to strengthen their powers over unsuspecting victims.

spittle of the hellhound, Cerberus, and any cases of monkshood poisoning were regarded as sorcery.

OAK – *Quercus robur*
Witches frequently held their meetings beneath oak trees, where they danced together at the stroke of midnight.

OATS – *Avena sativa*
Witches were reputed to collect as many as 20 or 30 male organs, often from men left to hang from the gibbet, and put them into a bird's nest, or shut them up in a box. The organs supposedly continued to behave as if they were still alive and the witch, under instructions from the Devil, fed them with oats or corn (maize). It is reported: '... for a certain man tells that, when he had lost his member, he approached a known witch to ask her to restore it to him. She

PEAR TREE – *Genus Pyrus*
Besides oak trees, witches often held their coven meetings under pear trees, similarly dancing beneath them at the midnight hour.

POPLAR – *Genus Populus*
Witches used the leaves of poplar trees in their flying ointments.

POPPY – *Papaver rhoeas*
Witches used the opium, present in the seeds of corn poppies, in their ointments, and ground them into powders to be burned during divinatory spells or to promote dreams of the future, also invisibility. The seeds were mixed with olibanum, cumin, alcohol, bay laurel, belladonna, hemp, henbane, mandrake, saffron and thorn apple. Opium was also used in a sleeping oil during the Middle Ages.

PURPLE ORCHIS – *Habenaria fimbriata*
Known as the Herb of Enticement, the

OPPOSITE: Witches used the oil of the olive tree for steeping herbs.

RIGHT: Poplar leaves were one of the ingredients in flying ointments.

LEFT: Saffron was used to make love potions, and is an expensive culinary herb.

OPPOSITE & PAGE 122: With about 500 species, speedwell or veronica is the largest genus in the family Plantaginaceae.

flying ointments and Irish fairies used the blossom to help them move around. In Cornwall, English witches used ragwort branches as vehicles for flying up to a high rock, known as Castle Peak, on moonlit nights. Because the fairies valued the plant, it was considered dangerous to damage or burn ragwort for fear of punishment. Ragwort is highly toxic to animals and must be removed from pastures.

ROWAN – *Pyrus aucuparia*
The rowan tree, also known as the mountain ash, was reputed to be able to cancel out the evil effects of witchcraft. To protect themselves, victims also wore rowan berries as necklaces, and believed they could be saved by touching the witch with a rowan branch.

RUE – *Ruta graveolens*
Witches used rue for its narcotic and hallucinogenic properties, combining it

purple orchis is also called satyrion, gethsemane, long purple, Cain-and-Abel – also dead men's fingers, ram's horns and crake feet. Witches used the plant as an ingredient of their love potions. The plant has two roots, which represent male and female. The larger root was used when a male was targeted and the smaller when it was a

female. The plant would have been picked before sunrise while the witch was facing south. Alternatively, the root would be ground up and used in other potions and ointments.

RAGWORT – *Senecio jacobaea*
Irish witches used this plant, which is also known as 'fairies' horse', in their

with a variety of other ingredients to make different potions.

SAFFRON – *Crocus sativus*

Cleopatra is said to have made herself irresistible to men by using saffron in her perfumes. It was also reputed to increase sexual desire in women, and was frequently used in magic love potions. Witches used saffron in ointments, often combined with other plants, such as hemp, poppy, and the thorn apple.

SCARLET PIMPERNEL – *Anagallis arvensis*

Also known as shepherd's clock, the plant was used by witches for its mild narcotic properties, and they would have taken potions of the pimpernel themselves, to help develop their power of second sight. Victims of enchantment may have used the plant as an antidote.

SCOPOLIA – *Scopolia carniolica*

Similar to belladonna and henbane in its action, witches used scopolia in their ointments and love potions. The plant was often spread over the floor at country dances, so that anyone dancing over it would be aroused. In the event of this highly toxic plant being ingested, disorientation, delirium, dilated pupils and an accelerated pulse rate are very likely to ensue.

SMALLAGE – *Apium graveolens*

This wild celery was mentioned in Nathaniel Hawthorne's short story of Puritan life, *Young Goodman Brown*, in which Goody Cloyse confesses to having used the plant to make her flying potions. She would possibly have mixed the smallage with cinquefoil, wolfsbane, fine wheat, and the fat of a newborn child.

SORGHUM – *Sorghum vulgare*

Documents relating to the Inquisition identify the fact that evil witches used the stalks of this plant in their nightly battles with the Benandanti, who used the stalks of the fennel plant to fight them off.

SPEEDWELL – *Veronica officinalis*

Also known as Paul's betony and prize of honour, it is said that in the event of

the plant being brought into the house, the mother of the family would die within the year.

ST. JOHN'S WORT – *Hypericum perforatum*
Although the plant is at its most potent around Midsummer's Day and the feast

The word hypericum *is Greek for 'above an icon', and the plants were hung above icons on 24 June, the feast of St. John the Baptist, to ward off evil spirits.*

123

THE WITCH'S GARDEN

LEFT: Tobacco was used by witches as an ingredient of love potions.

OPPOSITE: Some of the other ingredients of spells and potions.

TRAILING PEARLWORT – *Sagina decumbens*

Witches used the trailing pearlwort when preparing their love charms. They would gather together nine roots of the plant, knotting them into a ring. Then they held the ring in their mouths, while thinking of the person they wished to enchant. It would not be long before the victim succumbed to their spells.

VERVAIN – *Verbena officinalis*

Vervain or verbena has long been associated with magic and sorcery as well as with medicine. Witches used the plant frequently, and it was considered to be a sacred plant of the Roman goddess Diana, the Norse god Thor, and of the Druids. It is reputed to increase the power of magical tools when it is used to anoint them, and was used in ointments, brews, and love philtres. It was capable of rendering individuals invisible, had the power to impart physical strength, and also had

of St. John the Baptist, the plant was reputed to secrete a red oil from its leaves towards the end of August, when St. John was beheaded, and because it resembled blood, witches used it for magic purposes around that time. Today St. John's wort is thought to be an effective treatment for mild depression and anxiety.

SWEET FLAG – *Acorus calamus*

Also known as calamus, the sweet flag has scented leaves and rhizomes, and

was used medicinally as a psychotropic drug. Witches also used it in flying ointments, according to Reginald Scot's *Discoverie of Witchcraft*, that was published in 1584.

TOBACCO – *Nicotiana tabacum*

The dried leaves of the plant were used in smoking rituals by Native Americans long before it was introduced to Europe in the 17th century. Being mildly hallucinogenic, witches used tobacco in love philtres and potions.

LEFT & PAGES 128–129: The water lily was used in love potions and, paradoxically, was also given to monks and nuns to help them remain chaste.

aphrodisiac properties. It is said that vervain was used to staunch Jesus's wounds after he was taken down from the cross. Legend also says that it is a protection from vampires.

WALNUT TREE – *Juglans nigra*

As well as convening beneath oak and pear trees, some witches held midnight meetings under the branches of a walnut tree. Italian witches in Naples met under a certain walnut tree, located in Benevento, and witches in Bologna held their coven beneath such a tree on the night of St. John's Eve (Midsummer's Eve or the summer solstice).

WATER LILY – *Genus Nymphaea*

Also known as the 'flower of chastity', the water lily was used by witches in the preparation of magic love potions, and the white water lily was a popular means, used by medieval monks and nuns, of suppressing sexual desires and helping them to keep their vows of chastity.

WITCHES OF THE WORLD

The flowers would have to be plucked by a witch on a night when there was a full moon, but she would have plugged her ears first, to prevent the songs of the water fairies from bewitching her and dragging her into the water. The flower of the water lily was also used as a love charm, that would have been worn on the body.

WITCH HAZEL – *Hamamelis virginianus*

Witch hazel resembles the common hazel, which has been used since ancient times in water divining. These properties were recognized by early settlers in North America, who gave *Hamamelis virginianus* its common name, witch hazel, not because of its connection with witches, but because the Middle English word 'wych' meant pliant or bendable. Witch hazel is more commonly used to describe the astringent substance obtainable from the shrub's bark and leaves.

Famous in folklore for its magical properties, the common hazel (*Corylus avellana*) has long been held to have magical healing powers and it is still regarded in some parts as the sacred tree of the fairies, making it unlucky to pick cobnuts on the sabbath, for fear of summoning up the Devil. The god Apollo is believed to have given the caduceus, the herald's wand, to Mercury, which was made from the hazel and is a symbol of spiritual enlightenment and medicine.

Adam is said to have cut the rod of Moses from a hazel tree growing in the Garden of Eden, while St. Patrick was responsible for ridding Ireland of its snakes with a magic rod made from the hazel tree.

WOODBINE – *Gelsemium nitidum*

Highly poisonous, Scottish witches used the plant in magic rites in which they 'passed their patients nine times through a girth of garland of green woodbine'.

YARROW – *Achillea millefolium*

Also known as the holy herb, milfoil, sanguinary, and old man's pepper, among a great many other names, yarrow became infamous during the Lancashire Witch Trials, after a suspect admitted to using it to cure distemper and in divination. It was also used as a love charm, worn in a little bag about the neck, and was reputed to bring the wearer success in all things, including the practice of magic.

CHAPTER FIVE

THE WITCH-HUNTERS

*M*atthew Hopkins, the self-styled English Witchfinder-General, was active in East Anglia between 1645 and 1647, carrying out his self-appointed mission to root out witches and eradicate them wherever they could be found. During this short period, aided and abetted by his equally zealous assistants, John Stearne and Mary Phillips, Hopkins began what amounted to a reign of terror, bringing untold suffering and death to over 200 women, men, and even children.

Hopkins is by far the best-known of the witch-hunters, but there were many more, and each had their own methods of flushing out witches and extracting dubious confessions.

Witch-hunting techniques varied, and victims were often simply denounced by their neighbours before being passed onto the witch-hunters, who would use the most brutal methods imaginable to bring cases to criminal trial. Confessions were

extracted by means of hideous tortures, many of them having been learned from the Inquisition.

Suspects often died under torture, which was hardly surprising, seeing that many were already old, malnourished and sick. After the process of the law had duly taken place, and having been declared guilty, the witch would then be forced to face

certain death. The executions were public events, witnessed by the local people, court officials and witch-hunters. Once the sentence had been carried out, the witch-hunters were paid for their services, when they would move on to pastures new, where they would track down more witches.

On the day of execution, it was not uncommon for witches either to have their tongues removed or for a wooden gag to be placed in their mouths, and this despite the fact that they could obstensibly save themselves at any time, by renouncing Satan and returning to God. Death, in the majority of cases, was a foregone conclusion, which was

ABOVE LEFT: Matthew Hopkins, the self-appointed Witchfinder-General.

OPPOSITE: The pond at Mistley, Essex, where Hopkins ducked people to prove them guilty of witchcraft. They included ten men and women from Mistley and the nearby town of Manningtree.

not the case in Spain, where 'converts' to Christianity, from Islam and Judaism, would have been executed only if they relapsed.

In some countries, sexual sadism was very much the impetus informing the witch-hunters' techniques, rather than any real desire to get at the truth, and breasts and genitals were routinely mutilated with pincers, pliers and red-hot irons.

This seems to have been the case with the inquisitor, Foulques de Saint-George, who was denounced by the people of Toulouse after it was discovered he was imprisoning female suspects for his own purposes. By all accounts he was a serial rapist, choosing his victims carefully so that he could abuse them in the privacy of a prison cell, ostensibly with the support of the establishment

Despite the fact that some of the witch-hunters' activities were eventually curtailed, and some even suffered similar fates to those they had persecuted for many years, during the main witch-hunt periods, witches were blamed for virtually every ill that befell mankind. Acts of rebellion, questioning authority, failure to conform with the rest of society, and

LEFT: Mistley Church overlooks the ducking pond, and legend has it that events backfired on Matthew Hopkins, when he himself was accused of witchcraft and was ducked before being drowned. According to John Stearne, Hopkins's assistant, however, Hopkins died peacefully and was buried on private land in Mistley.

OPPOSITE: Manningtree was the small but charming town in Essex where Elizabeth Clarke, Sarah Bright, and six others, were accused of witchcraft.

particularly 'unexplained' calamities, were all signs that a person was a witch. Wherever political or religious turmoil existed, witch-hunts tended to become more intense, while in countries where the Catholic Church held firmer control, they were not usually as fevered or widespread. In some places, such as in Scotland, for example, witch-hunts were both severe and prolonged.

During the Reformation, witch-hunters ranged far and wide in their quest for witches. They were well-rewarded for their work, and the remuneration paid to witch-hunters by Inquisitional courts on the continent was particularly generous.

WITCHES OF THE WORLD

In Scotland, in the 17th century, it was the job of John Bain to prick the warts and other blemishes of suspects, in the belief that a 'Devil's mark' had no feeling and did not bleed. He was not content to stop at this, however, and eventually achieved a successful conviction himself, when he claimed to have clearly heard an old woman talking to the Devil, when passing her humble abode. Her defence was that she often talked to herself, because she lived alone, that she knew it was a foolish thing to do, but that she meant

OPPOSITE: Little remains of Old Chelmsford, Essex, other than its impressive cathedral. It was where Elizabeth Francis, Joan Waterhouse and Agnes Brown, known as the Chelmsford Witches, were apprehended and hung.

ABOVE: This woodcut depicts Matthew Hopkins accusing Elizabeth Clarke and her mother of having familiars, one of which was supposedly called Vinegar Tom, whose guise was that of a greyhound.

RIGHT: The Chelmsford Witches.

FAR RIGHT: Joan Waterhouse.

no harm. Even her neighbours supported her in her assertions, but Bain's evidence, because of his previous experience of witches, whom he claimed invariably muttered curses

conclusion that the woman would be found guilty and executed as a witch.

John Dick, and his associate, John Kincaid, were both witch-hunters and witch-prickers, but they were prosecuted in 1662 after they were denounced as frauds. Both were tried for 'deceit in their work of pricking witches for the Devil's mark'.

Matthew Hopkins, the self-styled Witchfinder-General, exploited the unrest of the English Civil War to prey upon the fears of the ordinary people.

At a time when the average wage was six pence a day, Hopkins received £23 for a single visit to Stowmarket, and £6 for one to Aldeburgh. According to King James I's (James VI of Scotland's) famous treatise on witchcraft, witches suckled their familiars, but given the predilection of the English for keeping pets, one can see why Hopkins chose this route as an easy way of obtaining convictions. In 1647 Hopkins published a pamphlet entitled the 'Discovery of Witches', in which he described his methods in sanctimonious and pseudo-legal detail. Fortunately he died soon after, and by all accounts 'in some disgrace', when

under their breath, was ultimately damning. When the woman's body was examined, it was therefore inevitable that some blemish or other would be found, which Bain presumably went on to prick until he found one that did not bleed, causing great pain to the suspect in the process. Sadly, it was a foregone

LEFT: Aldeburgh, Suffolk, now more usually associated with the English composer, Benjamin Britten and the Aldeburgh Music Festival, was where Matthew Hopkins carried out one of his notorious witch-hunts.

irate villagers drowned him in his own ducking pond.

John Stearne, who assisted Hopkins between 1645 and 1646, is quoted as saying that 'he personally knew of 200 executions that had taken place as a result of their workings'. It is not known how Stearne's career as a witch-hunter ended, but some tell of his involvement in a scandalous fraud.

The way witchcraft came to be treated as heresy in England began with the accession to the throne of the Catholic queen, Mary Tudor (Bloody Mary), who began to persecute Protestants in an attempt to return the country to Catholicism, after her

to Roman Catholicism, and wrote: '... we found in all places votive relics of the Saints, nails with which infatuated people dreamed Christ had been pierced, and I know not what small fragments of the sacred Cross. The number of witches and sorceresses had everywhere become enormous.' It is plain he saw no distinction between witchcraft and Catholicism, and it was not long before Elizabeth's Witchcraft Act was passed in 1563.

But Jewell's fanaticism failed to take root and only four women were hanged for witchcraft in his diocese: Elizabeth Stile or Rockingham, Mother Dutten, Mother Deuell, and Mother Margaret. By the time of Jewell's death in 1571, he had abandoned his extreme

OPPOSITE: The Alps, that bordered Italy, France and Switzerland, were also the scenes of notorious witch-hunts.

ABOVE: A woodcut depicting the Scottish Forfar Witches. Between 1661 and 1666, 42 people, mainly women, where arrested here and charged with witchcraft.

FAR RIGHT: A scold's bridle, used in the punishment of the Forfar Witches.

father, Henry VIII's defection from Rome. A Protestant, John Jewell, had accordingly fled England, arriving in Frankfurt-on-Main, Germany, in 1555, 'one of the most noted centres of witch-mania'. The following year he went to Strasbourg, another city that was similarly obsessed, returning to England in 1559 where, Queen Mary having been executed, he was made Bishop of Salisbury and 'one of Elizabeth I's most trusted advisers'. Jewell defended Elizabeth's opposition

LEFT: Woodcut of a witch in hell.

BELOW LEFT: The Malleus Maleficarum *was the witch-hunter's bible for around 250 years.*

BELOW: A woodcut from c.1600, showing a woman being ducked. The practice was also referred to as 'swimming'.

OPPOSITE: Witches hanging on the scaffold.

Calvinist position for the more moderate Anglican communion.

Heinrich Kramer and Jakob (James) Sprenger, Dominican inquisitors, had published a book in around 1486 called the *Malleus Maleficarum*, the Witches' Hammer, that was destined to become the handbook of witch-hunters, examiners, torturers and executioners for the next 250 years.

Two years earlier, Pope Innocent VIII had issued a notorious Papal bull on the subject of witchcraft, and this was used in the preface of *Malleus Maleficarum*, making it appear that the book's entire contents had been sanctioned by the Pope. The book lumped folklore, witchcraft and magic together, identifying witchcraft with devil-worship and hence with heresy, which consequently made it the concern of the Inquisition. As time went on, however, the authority of the book would ultimately be challenged.

The Inquisition was responsible for carrying out the work of the Roman Catholic Tribunal, responsible for exposing and punishing religious heterodoxy, and even after the power of the Inquisition began to wane, many continued to follow its example.

The Inquisition had emerged in around 1200, and to begin with was concerned with heresy, but the same techniques were used in the later witchcraft trials. It established the principle that accused witches were presumed guilty until they had proven their innocence. A conservative estimate suggests that over a period of 150 years, up to the end of the 16th century, the Inquisition caused the deaths of 30,000 so-called witches.

Agents of the Inquisition did much of the witch-hunting in France, and in what was to be a very early case, at a time when Hugues de Baniols was the inquisitor at Toulouse in 1275, Angèle de la Barthe was probably the first to be executed for witchcraft. She was found guilty of having eaten babies and cavorting with the Devil.

The witch-hunting judge, Balthasar Ross, operated in the Fulda area of Germany between 1603 and 1606. He was known particularly for his sadism and his use of red-hot skewers in extracting confessions. It is believed that he was directly responsible for the execution of 300 people, but Ross himself was eventually imprisoned, not for burning innocents, but for fiddling his expenses.

A prime example of witch-hunters operating together, to create something of an industry, took place in Bamberg. This was then a small German state and the persecutions began in around 1609, lasting until at least 1630. The Bishop, Johann Gottfried von Aschhausen, was responsible for the burning of around 300 people, 102 of whom were dispatched in 1617.

The Witch Bishop, Johann Georg II, operated alongside his Vicar-General, Bishop Friedrich Forner, and a council of Doctors of Law. They constructed a building, specifically to hold suspected witches, with room for 30 or 40 prisoners. Hundreds of suspects were rounded up between 1626 and 1630, and one of the council's number, Ernst Vasolt, executed at least 400 women.

The equivalent of Matthew Hopkins in Bavaria was Jorg Abriel, who was also Schongau's public executioner. Abriel was particularly active from the end of the 16th century to the beginning of the next, and over the years became rich and powerful by discovering witches in many German states. When he was unable to find a mark on a woman, he simply stated that she looked like a witch, and proceeded to torture her until she inevitably confessed.

Witch-hunters could either be proactive or reactive. Matthew Hopkins was an example of the former, in that he set out to find witches himself. Witch-hunters, such as those used by the Inquisition, tended to be reactive, responding to the requests of God-fearing Christians, who had sought their protection from witches and other evil beings.

Although the methods and techniques of witch-hunters varied, the aim was not only to identify potential suspects, but also to take an active part in extracting confessions from them, which resulted in many convictions, followed swiftly and inevitably by executions.

Toulouse, France. Angèle de la Barthe was the first to be executed for witchcraft here in 1275.

CHAPTER SIX
PROTECTION FROM
WITCHES

*M*any of the methods, whereby individuals protected themselves from witches, did not originate in the 16th and 17th centuries, but were of much earlier pagan origin, having been absorbed from Celtic, Scandinavian and Roman mythologies that had subsequently become mutated and adapted over the centuries. Others derived from folklore or superstition, or from stories handed down by parents to their children, to which following generations had added touches of their own. Many of these ideas held the vestiges of truth, and at a time when people were more religious, and at the same time more superstitious, it is easy to see how they would have believed, not only that witches existed but that such simple methods of repelling them would also be effective.

Protective devices, such as mummified cats and horse's skulls, have often been unearthed during archeological digs, and horseshoes and concealed items are still to be found in very old houses. Other methods are rather more difficult to pinpoint, having been taken from contemporary descriptions. For those who would question the fact that witches, the Devil, demons, fairies, and malignant spirits were once genuinely feared, other

BELOW: Many methods of protection from evil entities had early Celtic origins in Scotland (below) and Ireland.

OPPOSITE: Horseshoes placed in this position traditionally conferred good luck and protection from evil.

explanations need to be found as to why these protections were thought necessary. In those days, perhaps, people would have been less knowledgeable and tolerant, and people who were different in any way, being eccentric, odd in their behaviour, or who held unusual beliefs, could easily be misunderstood.

There would possibly have been lone or reclusive women, who capitalized on peoples' fears by terrorizing the locals so that neighbours would not bother them or steal their goods. Meanwhile, the bulk of the population, because natural phenomena were still imperfectly understood, would have seen any misfortune as a conspiracy to undermine their health, threaten their livelihood

RIGHT: In Norse mythology the ash tree was known as Ygdrasil or the World Tree.

OPPOSITE LEFT: The aspen, being associated with Christ's Crucifixion, is a power for good.

OPPOSITE RIGHT & PAGES 148–149: Birch was seen as cleansing and protective.

and livestock and cause deformities in their children. Most methods of protection were aimed at keeping witches at bay, rather than actively seeking them out.

AGRIMONY – Also known as cocklebur or sticklewort, a concoction made of agrimony, maidenhair fern, rue, ground ivy and broom straw was believed to produce perfect sight, probably because the Greek word, from which the word agrimony comes, indicates its use for eye conditions. The concoction was also used to identify and protect from witches, whatever their disguise.

ASH – The tree has close associations with Norse mythology, where it is known as Ygdrasil or the World Tree, whose roots and branches bound heaven, earth and hell together, its root

and evil spirits. Brewing the beer in eggshells avoided nightmares, especially those involving encounters with the Devil and his minions. One could also avoid finding that one's children had been stolen and replaced by demons, who would wreak havoc on a home.

BETONY – Also known as St. Bride's comb or bishop's flower, a sprig of

betony was often worn in the hat to confuse witches and ward off evil spirits.

BIRCH – Birch was considered to be a purifying or cleansing plant and was also used for protection. It was believed that a possessed person or animal could be exorcised of a demon by gently striking them with a birch twig. Traditional witches' brooms were often

being a source of virtue. Ash keys protected against evil sorcery, and ash wands were used to raise and focus healing energies and enchantments.

ASPEN – Its association with Christianity connects the aspen with anti-witch protection devices, because it was believed that the cross on which Jesus died was made of its wood, causing its leaves to tremble in shame and horror thereafter. It is said that aspen, placed on the grave of a witch, prevents her from rising and haunting those responsible for her death.

BEER – In Scandinavia, specially brewed beer was drunk to repel witches

made from birch twigs, and cradles were also made of the wood to protect infants from the evil intentions of witches.

BRAIDS – Braids were regarded as symbols of power and imbued with meaning, which made them valuable in rituals and ceremonies. In ancient Peru, turbans, slings and braids were used in burial ceremonies, along with wrapped/braided reeds and devices such as God's eyes amulets.

In Japan, braids were used in Buddhist rituals to edge and secure religious scrolls, while certain coloured braids were used to protect against witches and the evil eye.

BRASS – Brass was said to keep witches and evil spirits at bay, and cattle and other livestock often had bells made of the metal attached to ropes around their necks, to prevent them from the 'evil eye' and being possessed or killed by demons, witches or other evil manifestations.

BROOMS – A witch could not enter a house if a broomstick had been left inside the door. Old brooms were collected together, when they would be dipped in tar before each was set on fire.

OPPOSITE: Fires where lit in fields and the embers scattered to protect crops and livestock from witches.

ABOVE: It was traditional to put brass bells around cattle's necks to protect them from evil.

The burning brooms were then put in strategic places to protect animals and crops from witches and other such misfortunes.

BURNING – The object of this was to protect crops and livestock from sorcery intended to destroy their fertility. A fire would be lit and the embers scattered in the fields to flush out witches lurking there in the shape of hares or other animals. Such practices also increased the fertility of the land by burning off old growth.

A similar practice existed on the Isle of Man, where gorse was burned on the first morning in May. Trumpets and horns were blown at dawn, and guns were fired to frighten witches and fairies away from cultivated lands.

CANDLES – Vowing a candle to the Devil was a potent protection, and having made a gift of a candle to their master, lighting it would become a protection against witches.

CATS – Over time, the bodies of around 50 mummified cats have been found, particularly in old buildings, under floor-boards or in roof spaces, inside lath-and-plaster walls, or bricked up in cavity walls. Many were found to have been placed or to have died in hunting postures, as if about to pounce on a mouse. It is difficult to say whether their presence is deliberate or accidental, but some believe that the presence of cats, as magical beasts, was in itself a kind of counter-magic, designed to ward off witches' familiars and other evil spirits that might enter the building. Others believe that it was a ritual sacrifice, that would protect every person or animal living within the house.

CHARMS – Making or keeping charms was ill-advised when witch-hunting was at its height, chiefly because of their association with evil magic. But these could also be antidotes to evil, a means by which disaster and disease could be diverted. Making charms entailed the chanting of magic words, phrases, or prayers. Reciting the Creed, five Aves and five Paternosters was a charm of sorts, believed to be powerful enough to break evil spells, that had been cast on a person, their family or property.

CHICKENS – Curses returned to haunt those who uttered them, just as chickens always came home to roost. This led to the notion that chickens could be witches' familiars, and that if one had a choice between being possessed by an evil spirit or being molested by a witch, it was better that a chicken be sacrificed.

THE CHURCH GRIM – This was a benign spirit, often in the form of a black dog, that was thought to protect churchyards, which the Devil visited to

OPPOSITE: Vowing a candle to the Devil guaranteed safety from harm.

LEFT & PAGES 154–155: Good spirits in the form of black dogs protect graveyards.

claim the souls of people that had escaped him when they died. Witches were also interested in graveyards as a source of materials for their brews, potions and spells. The good spirit would continue to protect graves, but woe betide anyone unlucky enough to catch sight of it, when it would become an augur of the beholder's own imminent death.

The spirit takes the form of a black dog in Britain, but in Sweden it is a lamb, known as a *kyrkogrim*, while in Denmark it is a pig or grave-sow known as a *kirkegrim*.

DEER BONES – Deer bones have often been found in concealed places in Scotland. They were used in a similar way to horse skulls (page 160), found across England, Ireland and Wales.

DILL – Derived from the Old Norse *dylla*, meaning 'to lull' or 'soothe', this alludes to the plant's carminative properties. It was used as a charm

against witchcraft during the Middle Ages, its association with the craft stemming from its occasional mention in Celtic folklore, where it is known as *soyah* or *anet*. According to the ancient Celts, dill diverted a witch from her purpose or stripped her of her will to complete an evil deed. Wearing dill or rubbing it on one's body to leave its scent on the skin also protected a person from witchcraft.

GALLNUTS – In Wales, gallnuts or oak galls were suspended from kitchen beams and rafters to protect against Satan and witchcraft. This is because

ABOVE LEFT: A chicken could be sacrificed to protect oneself from possession by evil spirits.

ABOVE: Garlic traditionally deters vampires, also witches and evil spirits.

LEFT: Dill has the power to weaken a witch's will to do evil.

OPPOSITE ABOVE: Gemstones are believed to protect individuals from witches and the evil eye.

OPPOSITE BELOW: Hawthorn symbolized hope and the end of darkness.

rings was common, as was their incorporation into decorative artworks. Semi-precious coral or amber protected the wearer from the attentions of the Devil and his evil eye.

HAGSTONE – A hagstone is a pebble, found on a beach, through which the action of the sea has worn a hole. Hagstones were hung on bedposts to prevent nightmares, or they were hung in stables to prevent a witch from taking a horse and riding it to exhaustion, rendering it useless for work in the morning.

galls are associated with a bitter taste, which would have dissuaded witches from entering the house.

GARLIC – Garlic traditionally protected buildings and their inhabitants from vampires, demons, witches and the evil eye. Garlic was also worn around the neck, hung in a room, or used by healers as remedies.

GEMSTONES – The ruby, saronyx and cat's eye warded off evil spells, while pebbles, if scattered around the floor, were almost as effective. The inclusion of protective gemstones in bracelets or

cradles of newly-born infants as a protection against sorcery. Hawthorn was also useful as a deterrent against lightning strikes.

HAZEL – Hazel nuts were used as a protection against witches and all forms of evil, but paradoxically also in potion-making and casting spells. Double hazelnuts were useful for killing witches in Scotland, if thrown at them, while in other parts of Britain, cattle were branded with rods made from the wood of the hazel at Midsummer and Beltane, to ensure their safety from witches and fairies. Horses often had hazel wood incorporated into the breast bands of their harnesses.

HOLLY – Holly has religious associations, and the similarity of the words holly and holy makes the plant abhorrent to witches, the blood-red berries and the thorns being a reminder of Christ's death. A holly bush or large sprig of the plant, strategically placed, was thought to be a good way of dissuading anyone from entering a house, possibly because of the prickles.

HAWTHORN – A symbol of good hope, the flowering of the tree indicates that winter is nearly over and that spring is nigh. The tree was connected with witchcraft in Roman times, when branches of it were placed over the

HORSESHOES – Horseshoes are still thought to be a protection from witches

158

and witchcraft, while they prevent evil from crossing the threshold if placed over a doorway. Placing a horseshoe inside a chimney prevents flying witches from entering, and if nailed to a bedstead helps to prevent nightmares caused by witches. Once the horseshoe has been put into position, it must never be removed and its ends must always point down. If the horseshoe is intended as a good luck charm, the ends should be placed uppermost, otherwise the luck will fall out.

HORSE SKULLS – There appears to have been a widespread tradition in

Britain of concealing horses' skulls in places where large numbers of villagers regularly gathered together, such as the church or the local pub. It was thought that horses, like cats, had the ability to

OPPOSITE: This incorporates two protective charms, the horseshoe and blue eyes, to protect its wearer from the evil eye.

ABOVE: Hazel trees and their nuts were used in various ways to deflect evil.

LEFT: Holly, being associated with Christ's Passion, exerts a powerful force for good.

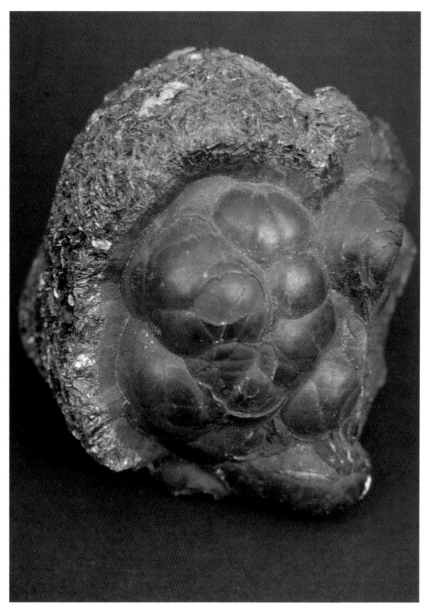

LEFT: Iron offered protection from demons and sorcerers.

OPPOSITE: Juniper was used as an aid to clairvoyance, in ritual purification, and to discourage witches.

see things that a human being could not, therefore the presence of the skulls was to frighten witches away by making them believe they would be detected, even though they were in disguise.

HOUSE LEEK – House leeks (stonecrops) were encouraged to grow on house roofs to protect their inhabitants from lightning, fevers and witchcraft. Charlemagne decreed that all should grow a form of this plant, known as *Jovibarba* (Jove's Beard), in the belief that it would protect the houses of his subjects from pestilence, and that evil spirits would also be discouraged.

IRON – Cold iron, a poetic and archaic name for iron, has traditionally been connected with magic, but any old iron knife, buried beneath a doorstep, could prevent a witch from entering a house. Iron was believed to be one of the best protections from evil spirits, demons, sorcerers and witches. Iron crosses were often used, but any item made of iron was an essential part of the construction of any building. In Sicily, iron amulets are popularly used against the evil eye, and horseshoes were thought to be particularly effective. Indeed talismanic properties are ascribed to most metals.

JUNIPER – Juniper wood is highly aromatic, when burned, and was used in ancient times for ritually purifying temples and to aid clairvoyance. The tree was also said to discourage witches in that they felt compelled to count its many needles before they could continue with their evil business.

LAVENDER – A sprig of lavender was worn to bring luck to its wearer. It was also capable of confusing witches and evil spirits, in that it made its wearer particularly alert to dangers emanating from those sources. It is also thought to promote restful sleep and can be used as a culinary herb.

WITCHES OF THE WORLD

PAGES 162–163: It was believed that lavender was capable of confusing witches and undermining their evil intentions.

OPPOSITE & BELOW: The tradition of making Halloween lanterns from vegetables and going trick-or-treating was brought to America by Irish and Scots immigrants.

LUCKENBOOTHS – These are heart-shaped brooches, worn as love tokens, or pinned to a baby's shawl as a protection against the evil eye. The name comes from the locked booths around St. Giles Cathedral in the Royal Mile in Edinburgh, Scotland, where the charms were originally sold.

LUNGWORT – The plant's oval, spotted leaves are said to resemble diseased lungs, so according to the Doctrine of Signatures, a form of sympathetic magic, it was used to treat lung conditions. It is associated with the Virgin Mary, and was worn as a protection from witches and evil spirits.

LEFT & OPPOSITE: Rosemary kept beer from going sour and protected breweries.

MAY DEW – Women went out before dawn to collect the May dew, or the first water from the well, which in Ireland was known as the 'top victory of the well'. This had potent magical properties and could secure good luck, a fair complexion, and protection from witches. In the wrong hands, however, it could be used to do harm.

MISTLETOE – Believed to cure diseases, make animals and human beings fertile, provide protection from witches, and bring good luck. The custom of kissing someone under the mistletoe comes from the Druid tradition of laying down arms beneath the mistletoe and exchanging greetings.

MUGWORT – Artemisia or mugwort was guaranteed to protect a house from all evil things. It was burned with sandalwood or wormwood during scrying rituals, and an infusion of the herb was drunk as an aid to divination.

PUMPKIN – Samhain was an ancient pagan Celtic festival, that marked the end of the old Celtic year. It became

The tradition that salt, once spilt, had to be thrown over the left shoulder, still persists.

synchretized with the Christian feast of All Souls or Halloween, on 31 October, in which Samhain rituals continued into modern times. Hollowed-out pumpkins or other vegetables, with candles burning inside, were placed in windows and porches to welcome the ancestral dead and repel evil spirits, particularly a restless spirit, known as Jack-o'-Lantern, who was denied entry to both heaven and hell. This also reflected the ancient Druid custom of lighting bonfires to protect against witches and spirits, who wandered abroad during the Samhain harvest festival.

ROSEMARY– An important culinary herb and a symbol of remembrance, rosemary was also regarded as a remedy for drunkenness. It was also added to beer to prevent it from going sour, and was believed to keep witches away from brewery cellars.

ROWAN – Pagan Britons valued the rowan, mountain ash, or wiggentree as a protection against enchantments, unwanted influences, and evil spirits. The Druids called the plant *witchen*, and used it to ward off witches.

RUE – This, the Herb of Grace, was used for sprinkling Holy Water over the persons or objects to be blessed. Rue is a bitter herb, associated with repentance, but when steeped in water it is a protection against contagious disease.

ST JOHN'S WORT – Believed to secrete a red substance from its leaves in August, when St. John the Baptist was beheaded, this was used by witches in their magical practices, because of its resemblance to blood.

In Italy, the plant is known as the Devil-chaser and it was woven into a bracelet in Germany to be worn on St. John's Eve, when witches took to their broomsticks. Wearing St. John's wort protected young girls from demons wishing to ravish them, and could also repel malignant fairies.

SALT – To avert evil, spilt salt must be thrown with the right hand over the left shoulder – a tradition that persists to this day.

Being a valuable commodity in ancient times, salt was used to purify and sanctify in Greek, Roman and Judaic rituals. It was also placed in coffins to signify immortality, incorruptibility, and to repel the Devil.

SCARLET PIMPERNEL – The plant's vivid colour associated it symbolically with blood, inevitably connecting it with the Crucifixion. In rural communities it was gathered to ward off witches and evil spirits, signifying that the household contained true Christian believers who must be left unmolested.

SHOES – Single shoes are often found concealed within chimney breasts or roof voids when old houses are being renovated. These are ritual objects, intended to prevent witches or evil spirits from entering the building. Two shoes are occasionally found, but they seldom make a pair.

SOW THISTLE – These plants exude a milky substance when any part of them is cut or damaged. They were once fed to lactating sows, in the belief that milk production would increase. Men also wore the plant, tucked into their hats or belts, to protect them from evil.

THYME – Thyme, besides being an important culinary herb, was also worn to protect from witches and fairies, and was scattered over the dead. Bunches of the herb were also thrown onto coffins, as a protection against evil spirits.

OPPOSITE: The rowan tree has the power to repel witches and their enchantments.

RIGHT: Thyme was placed on coffins at burials as a protection against the forces of evil.

TRAILING PEARLWORT – Carried as a protective herb, this was traditionally fed to cows to protect both their milk and calves. In Ireland, if placed above a door, it protected from the banshee, a wailing female spirit, who was regarded as a harbinger of death.

TREES – Specific trees, such as ash, aspen, hawthorn, hazel, holly, juniper, and rowan (see individual entries), were thought to be protections from the forces of evil

URINE – Urine is supposed to have magical properties. It was thought that a witch could be overpowered by obtaining some of her urine, or that a tile could be taken from the roof of her house, urinated upon, and adding salt before baking it in the oven. A bellarmine witch-bottle, discovered in 2001 beneath the hearth of an old cottage in England, was found to contain hair, pins, and traces of urine.

WITCH BOTTLES – Bellarmines are occasionally found concealed, not only beneath hearths and thresholds of old houses, but also beneath floors and in walls. Their most usual contents, used to cast spells, are iron pins or nails, human hair, small bones, thorns, pieces of wood, and fabric cut into the shapes of hearts. The bewitched could be recued, and the witch's power made ineffective, by drawing some of the witch's blood.

WITCH BOXES – These could contain pieces of human bone, herbs, and pieces of rowan over which a spell of protection had been cast. These boxes were frequently sold by witch-hunters, who would have acquired them while travelling from village to village.

YARROW – This has a variety of different names, including Devil's nettle, bad man's plaything, nosebleed, and the holy herb. Yarrow, whether used as a love charm or as a protection against witches, was worn in small bags around the neck.

PAGES 172–173 & LEFT: Various trees offered protection from witches.

BELOW: A bellarmine witch's bottle, heavily inscribed with magic symbolism, surrounded by its contents. These included pieces of bone and rusty iron nails, thought to be the means of casting magic spells.

CHAPTER SEVEN
EUROPEAN WITCHES

*E*urope was at the epicentre of the witch-hunt craze, but it is not known precisely how many people were accused, tortured, and subsequently executed for witchcraft. Each country has its own history of the events, as can be seen in the following accounts from 13 different countries.

The worst witch-hunts began in Austria during the reign of the Holy Roman Emperor Rudolf II (1576–1612), and were begun by the Jesuits as a way of dealing with Protestantism. The second period of persecution followed in the provinces of Styria and the Tyrol, beginning in 1678, and a vicious anti-witch code was adopted in 1707.

ABOVE RIGHT: Emperor Rudolf II.

FAR RIGHT: Leopold I.

OPPOSITE: The Stephansdom, Vienna. Austria's witch-hunts began before Rudolf II moved his court to Prague in 1583.

PAGES 178–179: A Styrian landscape.

Rudolf believed in witchcraft, but his main interest was the occult, his ambition being to find the Philosopher's Stone, that turned base metals into gold. Elizabeth I's astrologer, John Dee, who by now was also immersed in the occult, together with Edward Kelley, were also invited to Rudolf's court.

In 1583, the notorious trial at St. Barbara's in Vienna, initiated by the Bishop of Breisgau (Baden), saw an old woman accused of causing Anna Schlutterbauer to be possessed. After torture, the accused admitted a liaison with the Devil, raising storms, and attending Sabbats. Initially, she was judged insane, but this was overruled and she was condemned to be burned.

This approach persisted in Austria for the next 200 years, and suspects

found with oils, ointments or human bones in their possession were automatically arrested. In 1679, Emperor Leopold I forbade the introduction of new tortures, including the bed of nails, but between 1677 and 1681 at least 1,000 were tortured into making confessions, then beheaded, strangled or burned: the youngest was only ten, the oldest, 80.

In 1769, the Empress Maria Theresa limited the persecutions, in that no sentence for witchcraft could be carried out without the express permission of the government. In spite of this, however, some 30 different types of torture were still being used, and it was not until 13 January 1787 that the torture and burning of witches was at last outlawed.

In Austria where German was spoken, the guidelines for dealing with witches followed those of the Inquisition. A person never knew the facts and circumstances that had led to their accusation, and if they changed their confession after torture, they would be tortured again. Names of

Vienna saw the notorious trial in 1583 of an old woman charged with causing Anna Schlutterbauer to become possessed.

accomplices were wrung out of victims under 'moderate torture', in the interests of so-called accuracy, and interrogation always followed directly after arrest. This was to ensure that the Devil had no time to coach the witch. The torture chamber was sprinkled with holy water and fumigated with blessed herbs. Children under the age of seven were exempt from torture, but anyone over 14 was considered to be an adult.

As early as 1576, witches had been hunted in the Basque-speaking Pays de

LEFT: The Empress Maria Theresa limited the persecutions of witches in 1769.

BELOW LEFT: Many fishermen returning to Labourd, found their loved ones had been tortured and killed.

BELOW: Albrecht Dürer's 1519 portrait of Maximilian I. Maximilian introduced sweeping anti-witch laws that resulted in many persecutions.

Labourd, close to the Spanish border in France, and 40 or so were burned. Pierre de Lancre, a judge from Bordeaux, initiated new witch-hunts in the area in 1609, and in less than a year

LEFT: A woodcut, from the time of the Basque witch-hunts in France, depicting a Witches' Sabbat.

OPPOSITE: A Basque landscape.

Ferdinand, an archbishop and Elector of Cologne, had earlier approved a general Inquisition, between 1587 and 1589, when some 63 women were either beheaded or burned. In one instance, the Inquisition ordered a woman to be tortured continuously until she confessed, while another, having been accused of causing a hailstorm, was arrested, then tortured until she implicated others. These were similarly tortured, and all were eventually killed. In the small alpine town of Werdenfels alone, in a period of 20 month beginning in 1590, 49 women were burned out of a population of 4,700.

In 1597, William abdicated in favour of his son, Maximilian I. The Jesuit, Johann Baptist Fickler, brought his influence heavily to bear on the new ruler, having 15 years before advocated severe measures to eradicate witchcraft. Maximilian allowed himself to be convinced that witches were responsible for his wife's infertility, consequently, witch-hunting would be prolonged and

some 70 people were burned at the stake, among them several priests. De Lancre was still not satisfied, claiming that ten per cent of Labourd's population of 30,000 were witches and were still at large. Marie Dindarte (17) was tortured to reveal how she flew through the air, Saubadine de Subiette and her daughter told of how the Devil opened the windows through which they flew, and Father Pierre Bocal confessed to celebrating a Black Mass.

When the menfolk of the area returned from their fishing expeditions in Newfoundland, they discovered that many of their loved ones had disappeared, having been tortured and killed. This led to some 5,000 of them rampaging through the streets in a search for justice. De Lancre hastily changed sides, denouncing the witch-hunts to appease the rioters.

William V, the Pious, was Duke of Bavaria from 1579. His brother, Duke

LEFT: A witch being taken by a demon.

OPPOSITE: The Bavarian Alps.

encouraged his priests and judges to root out witchcraft wherever it might be found, and his *Instructions on Witchcraft* (1622) certainly rank among the most extreme treatises on the subject. The witch-hunts came to an end with the arrival of the Swedish invading armies in 1632, and eventually crop failure, being a common misfortune, was no longer blamed on witches. In 1666, however, a 70-year-old man was convicted of raising storms. He was tortured with red-hot pincers on three occasions before being burned alive.

A new surge of persecutions arose between 1715 and 1722, after a schoolteacher had been denounced. Caspar Schwaiger was accused by nine of his pupils of attending a Witches' Sabbat. Schwaiger persistently declared his innocence, refusing to confess despite being brutally tortured. He confessed after being tortured yet again, but later recanted. The second major trial of this sort, based on false accusations, took place in Moosburg in 1722, in which boys were again the accusers. This time the victim was Georg Prols, who was

severe during his reign. He introduced sweeping anti-witch laws in 1611, 1612 and 1622, his father, William V, having begun the process in 1590, both having been influenced by Jesuits. Eventually, the more moderate Jesuits among them were able to slow the persecution down, so that the year 1631 began to see a marked decline.

Maximilian's edict of 1611 states: 'All those who have made a pact with the Devil should be punished with torture, death by fire, and confiscation of property.' Maximilian positively

flogged and tortured before being beheaded. The 13 people he had been forced to implicate were later freed.

A year later, in 1723, Maria Walburga (22) was tried in a secular court in Mannheim as a witch. She was cleared and the judge concluded she was a common prostitute. However, the Episcopal court arrested her and tortured her until she confessed, after which she was burned. Some of the last trials took place between 1728 and 1734, when around 20 women were executed in Augsburg, at a time when burning alive was still the punishment for proven pacts with the Devil, and beheading for evil acts. The last documented execution took place in Swabia in 1775.

The Channel Islands held a unique position, being politically English while culturally French. Unfortunately, they adopted the worst of both approaches to the problem of witches. Their arrest and trial followed the more severe French practice and the English state confiscated the property of the condemned. At the time, Guernsey had only a few thousand inhabitants, and the conviction rate for witchcraft was disproportionately high.

OPPOSITE: King Charles I.

BELOW: King James I .

RIGHT: Guernsey, one of the Channel Islands, was the scene of trials for sorcery.

During the reigns of Elizabeth I, James I, and Charles I, some 58 women and 20 men were tried for sorcery in Guernsey. All but eight were convicted. Twenty-eight were hanged,

187

then burned, four were burned alive, one was banished (but was hung when she returned), four were whipped and had ears cut off, and 27 were banished from the island.

In Jersey, witches fared a little better. There were 66 trials between 1562 and 1736, with a conviction and execution rate of around half. There was no special law pertaining to witches on Jersey, but it was forbidden to seek assistance from them. Here, the typical signs that a witch was at work were lice on clothing, maggots in a bed, or a cow failing to produce milk.

Unusually, torture was used in the Channel Islands after a sentence had been passed, the intention being to confirm guilt before the death sentence was carried out, and it was also used to obtain the names of accomplices. Usually, the strappado was the preferred apparatus of torture, in which a victim was suspended in the air by means of a rope attached to their hands, which were tied behind the back. Weights would then be added in order to intensify pain.

In England, witches had been treated savagely for many years, going back to Anglo-Saxon times, and this continued to be the case throughout the medieval

Jersey fared better than Guernsey, but of the 66 tried, half were executed.

period. Malicious acts had to be proven, however, such as causing sterility, damage to crops, sickness and death. Originally, witchcraft was seen not as a crime against Church and state, but as an anti-social activity against one's fellow man. Witches could be banished, but causing death by witchcraft was a capital offence. Up until around 1300, witches were tried by ecclesiastical courts, before being turned over to secular courts for punishment. In 1371, a man found guilty of possessing a human skull was released after promising never to perform magic acts again.

In 1467, at a time when witches were being burned all over France, William Byg, a crystal-gazer, was simply sentenced to wearing a scroll on his head in public, stating his offence. This same approach pertained 100 years later, when eight men were released in 1560, after swearing never to dabble with sorcery again.

Treatment was entirely different if the accused was of noble birth, but sorcery was a serious matter in that it implied treason. Many were accused,

EUROPEAN WITCHES

LEFT: William Byg, found guilty of crystal-gazing in 1467, got off lightly.

OPPOSITE: Chelmsford Cathedral, England. The city was the scene of the famous Chelmsford Witch trials.

BELOW: Skeleton of an Osyth witch.

among the most famous being Queen Elizabeth Woodville and Jane Shore, the wife and mistress of Edward IV, who were accused of using sorcery to wither Richard III's arm. Both died natural deaths, but Jane was publicly humiliated for her crime.

Witchcraft came to be a more serious crime in 1563, when Elizabeth I, under pressure from the clergy, newly defined it as a heinous crime. With this came several notable trials of 'notorious' witches, including those of the Chelmsford Witches (1566), the Osyth Witches (1582) and the Warboys Witches (1593).

There were no barbarous tortures in England, but confessions were extracted with some brutality. Being forced to stay awake, the tying-up of limbs and a diet of bread and water were the most excessive treatments to which witches were subjected. Witches were not usually burned in England, this being reserved for traitors. Some, however, such as Marjery Jourdemain, did suffer this fate, having been found guilty of high treason in 1444; the fact that she was also a witch was incidental. The largest mass execution took place in 1645, when the 19 Chelmsford Witches were hanged.

Unique to English witches was the idea that the Devil's mark was upon their bodies, and few of the trials in the main witch-hunt period went without this accusation being made. The practice of witch-pricking, to find the Devil's mark, could easily be manipulated to prove that the Devil had sucked the blood of the accused.

Lasting for around 150 years from 1584, a debate continued in England as to the very existence of witchcraft, which would have been unknown and unthinkable on the mainland of Europe. Most English people were beginning to see witch trials as irregular, to say the least, and many openly opposed them.

James I came to the throne of England in 1603, having been James VI of Scotland and a firm believer in witchcraft. He became directly involved in the trial of the North Berwick Witches, who were made to confess that they had attempted to raise a storm to wreck the ship carrying James's bride from Norway. When the jury acquitted one of the accused, James flew into a violent rage and personally supervised the woman's torture. He followed this experience by writing his *Demonology*, in which he framed his approach to the handling of witches in the future. Over the years the king himself would

LEFT: Queen Elizabeth I brought in more stringent laws to deal with witchcraft.

OPPOSITE BELOW LEFT: Dante Gabriel Rosetti's Joan of Arc Kissing the Sword of Deliverance, *painted in 1863.*

OPPOSITE RIGHT: Jeanne d'Arc, painted in 1880 by Jules Bastien-Lepage.

become directly involved, sometimes removing cases from the judges' control.

Christianity came to Finland from Sweden in 1157, but pagan beliefs continued to persist here far longer than in many other European countries. Here, early references to witchcraft emphasize prophesying, sorcery, interpreting dreams and using charms. By 1573, witches and fortune-tellers were likely to be excommunicated and turned over to secular courts to be tried.

Successive Swedish rulers in Finland ordered witches to be whipped for their first two offences and then to be dragged in front of the judges. Special prayers to protect from witchcraft were read on Sundays and Holy Days, and the destruction of servants of the Devil by fire and sword was advocated.

Finnish laws roughly followed those of Sweden. Superstition was punished with fines, but actual witchcraft carried the death penalty. In 1683, the law stated that a man causing death to another by witchcraft would be hanged and a woman burned. Four years later, death would also be the fate of anyone found to have made a pact with the Devil.

According to records, the first trial for witchcraft in Finland took place in August 1595, when it was claimed that a woman had threatened to bring misfortune on others. Some of the accursed had seemingly fallen ill and the same woman later claimed that she could cure them. She was condemned to death, but it is not known if the sentence was ever in fact carried out. The town of Pohjanmaa became a

veritable hotbed of persecution, when 50 cases of witchcraft were tried in the 1650s, and this at a time when there had been only 11 other such trials in the rest of Finland.

In all, 50 or 60 people were tried and put to death for witchcraft in Finland, most of them women. Another surge of persecution occurred between 1666 and 1678, when the Finnish judges and clergy came heavily under the influence of German demonologists, and ten women were executed by burning in 1666. By 1734, although the death penalty for witchcraft was still in force, active witch-hunts had come to an end, and in 1779 the sentence was finally abolished.

There were five major periods of witch-hunting in France, the first being in the early 14th century, when the Inquisition identified witchcraft as a heresy. Joan of Arc was charged with heresy involving sorcery around the mid-15th century. The main period, however, was between 1450 and 1670, when witches were zealously hunted

Finland was known for its witches into modern times, in particular for the great shamans in Lapland. The pagan ritual of lighing bonfires on Midsummer's Night (above) still remains.

PAGES 196 & 197: Rouen. Joan of Arc was burned for witchcraft here, calling out the name of Christ. She was 19 years old.

195

out and trials and executions were at their height.

During the first half of the 17th century, nuns were often accused of being possessed by demons, while the French nobility began to come under fire for using poisons and attending Black Masses at the end of the 1600s.

From 1500 to 1670, barely a year passed without one or another witch being executed, many having been convicted for the death of people and animals. The actual cause of the deaths was ergotism, after grain infected with ergot, a fungus, had been ingested. There were mass trials in Béarn (The Basque Witches) in 1508, people were tried for lycanthropy in 1521, and 40 witches were burned in Toulouse 30 years later.

Delusions of witchcraft reached their peak in France from 1575 to 1625, when demonologists were allowed to influence judges presiding over trials. In Alsace, 102 witches were burned in the small village of Thann between 1572 and 1620, while in Lorraine the Attorney General, Nicolas Rémy, personally condemned 900 witches between 1581 and 1591. By 1596, 200 witches had died in St.-Amarin, and hundreds were burned in Normandy,

usually at Rouen, the periods of particular intensity being 1589–1594 and 1600–1645. At St.-Claude, the principal judge, Henri Boguet, launched

ABOVE: Louis XIV. Witch-hunts began to tail off in France during his reign.

RIGHT: Lyon. Here, Father Louis Debaraz's execution for witchcraft in 1745, was one of the last in France.

PAGE 200: Dijon (left) and Toulouse (right and page 201) both held witch-trials.

WITCHES OF THE WORLD

an intensive campaign against witches, and around 600 witches were executed.

Central areas of France tended to escape the mass terrors, although laws existed to prevent abuse and the parliament of Paris claimed jurisdiction over cases, including sorcery.

The witch-hunts in France began to draw to an end in 1682, when Louis XIV, while agreeing with the view that witchcraft was shameful, said that the term was misapplied through superstition and did not involve the Devil. Despite scattered trials being held over the next 50 years, when death sentences were passed, in practice the accused either died in prison or was banished. It is popularly believed that the last execution took place in Bordeaux in 1718, even though Father Bertrand Guillaudot was burned alive in Dijon in 1742, and there was another long and complicated trial in Lyon, which ended in 1745, when Father Louis Debaraz admitted to trying to locate treasure by magic means and was burned alive.

In stark contrast with England, where around 1,000 people were executed as witches, at least 100,000 were killed in Germany, and where torture was part of a process in which a woman was pitilessly tortured on 56 separate occasions.

During the main witch-hunt period, Germany consisted of around 300 autonomous states, each with their own laws, which individual rulers changed or enforced as they saw fit. The Lutheran Carpzov, known as the law-giver of Saxony, was said to have ordered the burning of 20,000 witches, and few would rival this figure. Some areas were also heavily influenced by Austria, Bavaria, and later on, Sweden.

Witch trials were not common until after 1570, when there was wholesale slaughter. In Quedlinburg, in Protestant Saxony, in 1589, 133 witches were burned in one day, while in the 22 villages under the jurisdiction of the Abbey of St. Maximin, outside Trier, 368 witches were executed between 1587 and 1594. Some 5,000 witches were burned in Strasbourg between 1615 and 1635.

It was during the Thirty Years War that persecution reached new heights. In 1629, for example, 77 witches were burned in Burgstadt, out of a

FAR LEFT: Strasbourg. Over 5,000 were burned for witchcraft here over a period of 20 years.

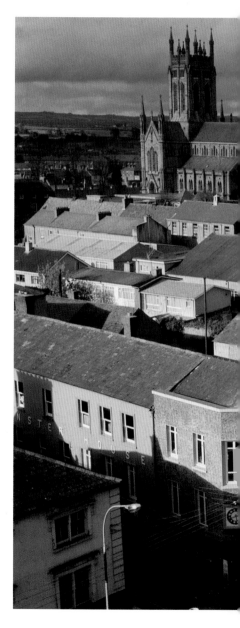

forbade the practice, hunting for witches began to diminish.

In Ireland, during the period 1324 to 1711, even when the witch-craze was at its height in Europe, no more than half-a-dozen witch trials took place. An odd trial, held at Kilkenny in November 1578, resulted in two witches and a 'blackamoor' being executed, and an old beggar woman was burned towards the end of the 17th century, when she was claimed to have caused a young girl to vomit needles, pins, hairs and feathers.

The earliest recorded witch trial in Norway took place in 1592, but throughout its history, only around two dozen witch trials were held, even though a woman killed herself in prison while awaiting trial in 1622.

There was a major trial in 1650, when Karen Thorsdatter admitted being in the service of someone called Lucifer. She implicated several others, who in turn admitted to raising storms and being able to fly. At least two

population of less than 3,000. In 1608 a man died in prison from the effects of torture; his wife was hoisted in the strappado 11 times, and their 21-year-old daughter was tortured the same number of times, with a 50-lb weight attached to her legs. Another common torture was the use of the Spanish boot, designed to crush the feet and legs.

A factor that appears to have motivated witch-hunting was the prospect of confiscating a witch's property, and once the Emperor Ferdinand II (1619–37) eventually

ABOVE LEFT: Emperor Ferdinand II.

RIGHT: Kilkenny, Ireland. Two witches and a blackamoor were executed here in 1578.

EUROPEAN WITCHES

LEFT: James VI of Scotland.

BELOW: Mary, Queen of Scots.

RIGHT: Bilbao, Spain. Although the belief in Basque witches was widespread here, the Spanish Inquisition preferred to persecute Protestants and the baptized descendants of Jews and Moors.

usually involving treasonable acts, including sorcery used against the king. The recognition of witchcraft as a crime, however, came in 1563, with a new act introduced by Mary, Queen of Scots. After that, there was a trickle of cases, and several were burned before King James VI of Scotland's accession to the throne in 1567.

of them were sentenced to burn in Kristiansand, and seven witches were burned in the same area in 1670, having confessed to poisoning people, flying, and attempting to destroy ships.

Probably the last witch trial took place in Norway in 1684, when a man called Ingebrigt admitted he had sworn allegiance to the Devil, after having walked three times backwards around a graveyard. He had also tried to poison cattle and despite later retracting his confessions, he was burned alive.

Scotland is only second to Germany in terms of barbarity. There was a series of trials of people of noble birth,

The worst periods of persecution were from 1590 to 1593, 1640 to 1644, and 1660 to 1663. Torture was permitted and prisoners were kept awake, lying naked on cold stone, and many were forced to wear hair shirts steeped in vinegar. Vices were used to crush arms and prisoners were pressed beneath iron bars and forced to wear Spanish boots.

The probable end of Scottish witchcraft took place in 1727, after a case involving Janet Horne, who was accused of using her daughter as a flying horse, and was burned in Ross-shire. In all probability around 4,400 witches were burned in Scotland in the main period 1590 to 1680.

Although the Inquisition was highly active in Spain, the country was actually spared many of the horrors of the witch-hunts. There were a handful of cases before 1526, including three women executed in 1500, and 30 were burned in Biscay in 1507.

There were, however, two major outbreaks, one in Navarre in 1527, the other in Biscay in 1528, which the authorities quickly suppressed, in the belief, unlike the Inquisition, that

A Swedish port. Eighty-five people were burned for witchcraft in Sweden.

witchcraft was simply an illusion. Spain was certainly affected by the persecution of the Basque Witches in 1609, but even the Spanish Inquisition refrained from persecuting old women in their 70s and 80s.

By 1611, the Spanish government was allowing accused witches to repent without penalty, and as long as they gave evidence and made confessions they would be spared. There were a handful of trials between 1622 and 1641, but no one was convicted. In fact no individual in Spain was executed for witchcraft after 1611.

The most significant series of witch trials in Sweden took place at Mora in 1669, and resulted in the burning of 85 people, who were convicted of teaching children to fly.

More witches were beheaded or burned in the period 1674 to 1675; in fact, it may have been as many as 71, the prosecutions having been made possible by laws dating back to the beginning of the 17th century. Accusations of sorcery had to be substantiated by six witnesses, and the death penalty for this crime remained in force until it was abolished in 1779.

The Swedish Queen Christina believed that women who confessed to having made pacts with the Devil were either mad or suffering from delusions; in a letter written by her in February 1649, it clearly indicates that the witch-hunts should end. And indeed they did, for Christina banned all witch trials, not only in Sweden but also in Sweden's possessions elsewhere.

Witchcraft had always been a virtually impossible crime to prove, despite the fact that many people were convicted of witchcraft and executed. For centuries, guilt was proven on the basis of cause and effect; for example, a woman would have an argument with her neighbour, following which the neighbour's cow would die and its owner would cry witch. It followed, therefore, that the accused, in order to have performed this act, must have been in league with the Devil.

Witch-hunting was a self-perpetuating business, and so that witch-hunters, judges, lawyers and priests might be continually employed, accused witches were forced to give or invent the names of accomplices, who in turn would be tortured to reveal more names.

There were few places in Europe where witchcraft was resoundingly rejected, both as a crime and as a concept, apart from the Duchy of

BELOW: Queen Christina of Sweden.

OPPOSITE: A Scottish landscape. The last to be burned here was Janet Horne.

Juliers-Berg, where not a single witch was burned between 1609 and 1682. Holland was the first in Europe to outgrow feudalism and after 1610 no one was killed, but in France it took until 1682, when an edict of Louis XIV ended the witchcraft trials. Commerce could not live in a world of uncertainty and the witch-hunts were undoubtedly responsible for the climate of fear.

CHAPTER EIGHT
WITCHES OF THE WORLD

The concepts of sorcery and witchcraft seem to have persisted into modern times in many parts of the world. In some African cultures, it is still believed that covens of cannibal witches can be found, sitting around fires, sometimes in graveyards, where rather like vampires, they drink blood extracted from their victims. They are supposedly able to take the soul from a victim's body and keep it, so that the victim eventually dies.

This example illustrates the fact that views on witchcraft have changed very little from those held during the 16th and 17th centuries, in that witches are believed to have powers to do evil because of their pact either with the Devil or an evil spirit. African witches are also reputed to have animal familiars that are typically wild animals, such as hyenas or baboons.

Proving witchcraft is no easier now than it was all those years ago. The witch is supposed to have an evil spirit housed within their stomach, which increases its power and the range of its

abilities as the witch gets older. It is through this power that the witch is able to create spells and potions.

Given the fact that Africa has an enormous number of traditional

OPPOSITE: Terrifying images of demons can be seen at Fengdu, China's Ghost City.

ABOVE & RIGHT: Witches in Africa have wild animals as familiars, such as hyenas and baboons.

religions, it is hardly surprising that vestiges of these religions should remain in many parts of the continent. Africa is not, however, the only place to retain elements of witchcraft.

In some African cultures the witch is believed to act in an unconscious

LEFT: Kilimanjaro, Tanzania. Witchcraft is still practised in Tanzania, for which two football clubs were recently fined.

ABOVE: More often than not, African witch doctors make use of natural remedies rather than magic powers.

215

manner, unaware of the fact that they are causing harm. Sickness, death, crop failure and other misfortunes are still laid at the door of witches, and they are even blamed for epidemics and natural disasters. Even today there are widespread confessions of guilt.

In Brazil, for example, the loss of a job is more often than not put down to witchcraft rather than more ordinary reasons. In fact, the belief in witchcraft exists throughout South America, often co-existing with strong Christian beliefs. Here, as elsewhere, accusations of witchcraft tend to occur when there is no direct, rational reason for a calamity or misfortune, or there is a sudden disappearance, a mysterious death or sudden changes in the climate.

In parts of Chile, it is said that the connection of witches with evil forces gives them the ability to harm others or gain advantages for themselves. At the same time, however, these same women are routinely consulted, and provide herbal remedies for both human beings and their animals.

LEFT: Objects used by Zimbabwean witch doctors.

OPPOSITE: Voodoo dolls in Togo.

It is not surprising, therefore, that in a country such as Ghana, where animist religions co-exist with Christianity and Islam, and where some of the world's poorest people live, that witchcraft is said to be alive and well. Africans, when sick, tend to consult both medical and witch doctors, using the former to treat physical conditions and the latter, because of their powers of divination, to discover their underlying cause. Witch doctors are also believed to be able to protect individuals against the negative supernatural powers of their enemies.

Accusations of witchcraft technically became illegal with the arrival of the Europeans in continents such as Africa, but since independence, many of these laws have been reversed.

Nowadays, although there are cases of witches being murdered, it is rather more likely to see them banished from their villages or forced to live on the fringes of society. Today, the term witch-hunt means something rather different, and is more often applied to campaigns directed at groups, whose views are considered to be at odds with the status quo.

The belief in witchcraft is not only restricted to cultures maintaining their

traditional customs and beliefs, but also exists in industrialized countries, such as Japan, where witches are believed to have owls as familiars.

Perhaps one of the most striking examples of witchcraft can be seen in Haiti, where the practice of voodoo is a peculiar mix of traditional African culture and Roman Catholicism. Voodoo is believed to have originated in West Africa, where it was used to explain the forces of nature and human behaviour, which, as a result of the slave trade, spread to North and South America as well as to the Caribbean. Voodoo became the official religion of Benin in 1996 and is believed to be still practised by around 30 million people across West Africa. Voodoo itself is unreasonably linked with Satanism, zombies and voodoo dolls, that arose from the Haitian practice of nailing such dolls to trees, near cemeteries, to

OPPOSITE & ABOVE: A market in Togo, where witch doctors can obtain fetishes and the ingredients for making their potions, that include monkey skulls, warthogs' teeth, crocodile skin, and sometimes even human remains.

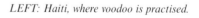

LEFT: Haiti, where voodoo is practised.

ABOVE: A voodoo doll with nails.

PAGE 222: A Haitian voodoo painting of faceless people.

PAGE 223: A market in Haiti.

relay messages from this world to the next. Voodoo as a religion places a firm emphasis on ancestors and the spirits of family members who have died.

A bizarre event took place in Tanzania in November 2006, and illustrates the fact that witchcraft is still very much alive. Officials from two of Tanzania's top football clubs, Yanga and Simba, were said to have performed witchcraft before a game, and the Tanzanian football federation fined both clubs. Indeed, the belief in witchcraft is so widespread in Tanzania that the big teams often hire witch doctors to accompany them to key matches.

There was another incident in the south-eastern Indian state of Andhra Pradesh in August 2003, when several villagers, suspected of being witches, were burned alive, and the epidemic is thought to have spread to around 130 villages in the area. Indian officials put the problem down to illiteracy and ignorance, but only the year before, worshippers at the Kamakhyat Temple in Assam had been accused of reviving the practice of human sacrifice, when it is thought that the last time this occurred was in 1796. There were other incidents of witch-hunting in 2002 and

OPPOSITE: Devotees of the Kamakhyat Temple, Assam, were recently accused of reviving the practice of human sacrifice.

LEFT: A witch doctor treating a patient.

BELOW: An African fertility charm.

in 2003, the second case in Jharkhand involving three members of the same family, who committed suicide after they were accused of causing the death of a person by casting spells on him. There were more such killings in Assam in 2006, when at least five people were murdered in two separate incidents. It was at this point that the Indian police admitted that in the five years up to 2006 around 200 people had lost their lives, allegedly as a result of witchcraft.

In the same year, Zimbabwe, rather bizarrely, decided to lift its ban on witchcraft, the laws having been passed in colonial times, to allow traditional healers to operate more openly. The Church in Zimbabwe has always believed that witchcraft existed in the country, and the new laws stipulate that proof has to be provided that an individual has used supernatural powers to harm others.

OPPOSITE: The Philippines, where witchcraft is also used as a power for good.

RIGHT: A Native American Hamasta shaman.

PAGES 228–229: A Zambian witch doctor.

knowledge of the moon and the occult.

Many cultures exist in South East Asia, and spells, divination, protection rites, shamanism, and dancing ceremonies are common practices.

Magic, witchcraft and the belief in spirits also play an integral part in the lives of the people of the islands of the South Pacific, where spells are cast to ensure bountiful catches of fish and exotic shells are used as charms. The Aboriginal people of Australia believe in a kind of natural magic, in which everything around them is thought to have been created in the Dreamtime, making the land particularly sacred.

Mangkukulam is the Filipino word for witch or sorcerer, and the words *brujo* or *bruho*, presumably from the Spanish, are used to describe warlocks, and *bruja* or *bruha* witches. It is believed that a *mangkukulam* can recite (*kulamin*) a spell (*sumpa*) to make an individual suffer pain, but can also be used for positive means to deal with certain illnesses and diseases. Herbal practitioners are called *albularyo* and

Witchcraft in China forms an integral part of traditional mysticism, religion and art. There is a huge body of Chinese literature on magic, the occult properties of plants, and on astrology and clairvoyance. Chinese witches have close associations with books, staffs, rabbits as familiars, and

ABOVE LEFT: A Native American medicine man.

OPPOSITE: A witch doctor's grave.

Images on Indian Doctor's Grave, Chilkat, Alaska.   Copyright 1895 by Winter & Pond.

people in rural areas rely on them completely to cure their ills.

Witchcraft and magic have long been practised in Eastern Europe. In Russia witches are known as *vedma*, the word deriving from the old Russian word, *ved*, meaning knowledge. The Russians believed that a woman could be born a witch or could become one as she got older. They also believed that witches had to establish a relationship with the Devil in order to obtain secret knowledge, and that a sign that this had occurred usually took the form of a mole or a wart. There was no major witch-hunt in Russia, although some were burned alive in Pskov in 1411.

Prior to the arrival of Europeans in America, Native American witchcraft was widespread, which involved rituals performed to induce visions, the wearing of masks and costumes, amulets and charms. At first, Europeans misunderstood the traditional role of Native American medicine men, who are herbalists and faith healers rather than magicians.

AMERICAN WITCHES

When one thinks of witchcraft in the United States, a country born out of the rebellion of the English colonies on America's east coast in 1775–83, the name Salem springs immediately to mind. In America, however, where some 36 individuals were executed, witch-hunts were sporadic and could even be described as mild, compared with what was happening in 16th- and 17th-century Europe.

The witch trials themselves were confined to the English settlements of New England, and there were only a few minor incidents elsewhere. In 1684 a distinguished Puritan, Increase

Mather, a major figure in the Massachusetts Bay Colony and the father of the equally influential Cotton Mather, had published a lengthy treatise, supporting the existence of apparitions, witches, diabolical possessions and 'other remarkable judgements upon noted sinners'. In May 1692 Increase returned from England, accompanied by a new governor for the colony, Sir William Phips, having renegotiated the colony's charter. The two arrived to find the

small village of Salem in the grip of mass hysteria. Increase Mather would later be criticized for his delay in putting a stop to the trials, given his own considerable moral authority.

Cotton Mather (left), the son of Increase Mather, would also be influential in the affairs of Massachusetts Bay Colony. His grave is pictured above.

OPPOSITE: Confession of Salem Jurors, 1692.

Puritan ministers believed that anyone connected with Satan was guilty of treason, not only against God but also the colony. They also believed they had uncovered a plot to destroy the village, beginning with the house of the minister, the Reverend Samuel Parris, and that the subsequent destruction of the church would herald the creation of Satan's kingdom upon earth.

Bearing in mind that the last witch had been executed in England in 1685, it was not surprising that panic broke loose when the blame for causing men, women and children to sell their souls to the Devil was laid at the door of a group of unmarried women, all of whom had visited the minister's house.

In January 1692, two young girls, Elizabeth Parris and Abigail Williams, the daughter and niece of the minister, began to scream blasphemously, throw things about the room, suffer convulsive fits, and complain of being pricked with pins and cut with knives. Shortly afterwards, other girls in Salem began to exhibit similarly abnormal behaviour.

Their doctors, being unable to account for their behaviour, concluded they were under the influence of Satan.

CONFESSION OF SALEM JURORS, &c.

From Calef's "Salem Witchcraft." Page 294.

" Some that had been of several Juries, have given forth a paper, signed with their own hands, in these words:

" WE whose names are under written, being in the year 1692, called to serve as jurors in court at *Salem* on trial of many ; who were by some suspected guilty of doing acts of witchcraft upon the bodies of sundry persons.

" We confess that we ourselves were not capable to understand, nor able to withstand the mysterious delusions of the powers of darkness, and prince of the air ; but were, for want of knowledge in ourselves, and better information from others, prevailed with to take up with such evidence against the accused, as on further consideration, and better information, we justly fear, was insufficient for the touching the lives of any : Deut. xvii. 6., whereby we fear we have been instrumental with others, though ignorantly and unwittingly, to bring upon ourselves and this people of the Lord, the guilt of innocent blood ; which sin the Lord saith in scripture, he would not pardon : 2 Kings xxiv. 4 ; that is, we suppose in regard of his temporal judgment. We do therefore hereby signify to all in general (and to the surviving sufferers in special) our deep sense of, and sorrow for our errors, in acting on such evidence to the condemning of any person.

" And do hereby declare that we justly fear that we were sadly deluded and mistaken, for which we are much disquieted and distressed in our minds ; and do therefore humbly beg forgiveness, first of God for Christ's sake for this our error ; and pray that God would not impute the guilt of it to ourselves nor others ; and we also pray that we may be considered candidly, and aright by the living sufferers as being then under the power of a strong and general delusion, utterly unacquainted with, and not experienced in matters of that nature.

" We do heartily ask forgiveness of you all, whom we have justly offended, and do declare according to our present minds, we would none of us do such things again on such grounds for the whole world ; praying you to accept of this in way of satisfaction for our offence ; and that you would bless the inheritance of the Lord, that he may be entreated for the land.

" Foreman, THOMAS FISK,
WILLIAM FISK,
JOHN BACHELER,
THOMAS FISK, Jun.,
JOHN DANE,
JOSEPH EVELITH,
THOMAS PERLY, Sen.,
JOHN PEBODY,
THOMAS PERKINS,
SAMUEL SAYER,
ANDREW ELLIOTT,
HENRY HERRICK, Sen."

[Not dated.]

The girls were questioned, following which the first to be accused were Sarah Good, a pipe-smoking beggar, Tituba, a slave, Sarah Osborne, a disabled woman who had been married three times, and Martha Cory, who had a mixed-race illegitimate son. All fitted the accepted stereotype of a witch, and no one was likely to stand up for them. But more ominously, neither Good nor Osborne ever attended church.

Most of the girls had fits in the presence of the accused, while, in court, their sworn depositions were strangely similar, all claiming to have seen visions of those who had afflicted them. Captain John Alden of Boston, a well-respected sea captain, who had fought in the Indian Wars, was also named as a witch. When brought into court, the girls fell flat on their faces, but as soon as Alden touched them were seen to recover. Alden was imprisoned in a Boston jail, but was able to escape 15 weeks later.

LEFT: The Witch Museum, Salem, Massachusetts.

OPPOSITE: A young girl fainting in the presence of a 'witch', during the Salem Witch Trials.

Darley

As the number of accusations grew, so the prison populations of Salem, Ipswich, Charlestown, Cambridge and Boston began to swell. Trials were being delayed because the newly-appointed governor and the new charter for the colony had not yet arrived from England.

In the end, many of the accused were sentenced to death, not because they admitted to being witches but because they denied it. Realizing that a confession meant a reprieve, Tituba also confessed and 55 out of the 150 who had been accused saved themselves in this way. Tituba, after spending 13

months in prison, was sold to recover expenses due to her imprisonment.

During the course of 1692, 31 individuals were sentenced to death, 19 of whom were hanged. Two died in jail, one was pressed to death, one was held indefinitely in jail without trial, and two claimed to be pregnant. One

escaped from jail after they had been sentenced, and five secured reprieves by making confessions.

The son of Increase Mather, Cotton Mather, was of the opinion that the cases had been dealt with in a far more lenient and impartial way than those in England. But while this may have been true, confessions were being forced out of the accused by binding their necks and heels until blood came out of their noses, while others were being subjected

ABOVE: The Ducking Stool, an illustration by Charles Stanley Reinhart. RIGHT & PAGES 238 & 239: The Witch House, once the home of Judge Jonathan Corwin, is the only building connected with the Salem Trials of 1692 that still remains.

to intensive questioning and denied access to lawyers.

Eventually, the general populace would be divided as to whether or not the case for witchcraft had actually been proved, and why some girls had been bewitched while others had not. There was also the question of why some highly-placed individuals, who had also been accused, were not prosecuted. In October 1692, Increase Mather published 'Cases of Conscience Concerning Evil Spirits', in which he stated that 'It were better that Ten Suspected Witches should escape, than

that one Innocent Person should be Condemned'. Only one more trial was conducted before those who were still in prison, in May 1693, were set free.

Much later, in 1711, the judgements against 22 of those who had been convicted in 1692 were reversed, which was of little comfort to the families of those who had already met their deaths. Around two dozen of the accused or their descendants had been seeking financial compensation for their losses, but in the end, although the claims were admitted, only £600 was allocated to be divided among all.

Although the rest of the United States did not suffer the same hysterical outbreaks as those occurring in New

OPPOSITE: *The kind of scene that was typical of the Salem Witch Trials.*

RIGHT: *An elderly woman, accused of witchcraft, being led away during the Salem Witch Trials.*

England, there had been a few isolated incidents. Some years before, in 1685, Rebecca Fowler was the only one of five witches prosecuted in Maryland to have been hanged, while in Princess Anne County, Virginia, in 1706, Grace Sherwood was tried for witchcraft but released, and convicted witches were punished three years later in South Carolina. Connecticut executed four witches, including Alse Young, who was probably the first ever to be hung for witchcraft in America in 1647.

During the period 1648 to 1691, around a dozen witches were executed in New England before the onset of the Salem Trials, while several others were banished or whipped. New York did not suffer the same delusions of witchcraft, but Rhode Island, despite having no trials, did have witchcraft laws. Jane Wellford was convicted in Dover, New Hampshire, in 1656, but was later freed on the grounds of good behaviour. In 1669 she sued the courts

THE ARREST.

OPPOSITE: One of Salem's patriarchs, George Jacobs, ridiculed the trials, following which he too was accused, tried, and executed.

BELOW: The Witchcraft Memorial, in Danvers, Massachusetts, commemorates the people who were executed during the Salem Witchcraft Trials of 1692.

and her accusers and was awarded £5 plus costs.

In Pennsylvania in 1684, Governor William Penn personally intervened to direct the juries to acquit alleged witches in two trials. It is believed that had it not been for this, a similar anti-witchcraft movement would have exploded among the Swedish and German populations of the colony.

Most of the rest of the trials took place in Massachusetts. Margaret Jones, a herbalist, was hanged in Boston in June 1648. She had fallen out with her neighbours and on examination was found to have a Devil's mark. She was sentenced to death for bewitching children.

IN MEMORY OF THOSE INNOCENTS
WHO DIED DURING THE
SALEM VILLAGE WITCHCRAFT HYSTERIA
OF 1692

WITCHES OF THE WORLD

In Springfield, in 1652, Hugh Parsons and his wife were accused of witchcraft. The husband was found not guilty but his wife was convicted. In 1656, a Mrs. Hibbins, the sister of Governor Richard Bellingham, was charged with witchcraft and was hung in June that year. But during the period 1660 to 1680, most of the witch trials were dismissed; by now, the appetite for hunting witches had fortunately diminished; Margaret Read did not even appear to answer charges against her at Ipswich in 1680, and the court made no attempt to issue a warrant for her arrest.

The last woman to be hanged in the city of Boston was Goody Clover, an Irish immigrant, who met her end on 15 November 1688. Probably the last trial in Massachusetts took place in 1693, again in Ipswich, after Sarah Post of Andover had been accused of having 'made covenant with the Devil and signed the Devil's book'. She was acquitted of the charge.

In 1985, in the District Court of Virginia, the Wicca religion was legally recognized as such and afforded the benefits of protection by the law. Wicca is a pagan religion and approximately 150,000 Americans

FAR LEFT: The Charter Street Cemetery is the oldest in Salem. It contains the graves of a Mayflower pilgrim and John Hathorne, one of the judges in the Salem Witch Trials. A memorial was also dedicated here in 1992, to commemorate the 300th anniversary of the strange occurrences in Salem in 1692.

identify themselves as Wiccans. It was probably in the 1950s that Wicca began to grow popular, after the British Witchcraft Act was repealed. Wicca, however, is only one aspect of modern-day witchcraft, and Wiccans organize themselves into covens, presided over by priests and priestesses. Nowadays, the Wicca religion is styled on Victorian cultism, interspersed with a mix of old pagan religions and with Buddhist and Hindu influences.

It seems that with the legal acceptance of the Wicca religion, witchcraft has come full circle. It was an accepted part of life before the rise of Christianity, but in the interim has spent centuries underground. Once subjected to persecution, it has now emerged as a vibrant religion, complete with its own particular code of ethics.

7. The Fetch

PSYCHIC DOUBLE OF A PERSON FORE-
ING, HEALTH OR IMPENDING DE

A lso known as a wraith, the fetch is the special app
a person, believed to presage that person's death and
people have an uncanny premonition of their death and d
telling them. Based on the knowledge, the fetch image is
a person to gain understanding that a person may unconsciou
... through the desire to communicate before they pass over, to t
... as with a wave before passing on to the Otherworld.

... described as a visible representation of a person's sou
... for the purpose of visiting the astral plans, warning
... positive spell.

... there doubles can be found in paintings that
... light that surrounds the whole body), ha
... only), or shadow, such as is seen in the fa
... "How they Met Themselves," w
... doppelgangers. These others bodies
... form or more clearly as in Kilber
... believed that the stranger o

Spirit doubles can seem quite separately from its host, but to view your own fetch is usually an omen of impending death.

At the time of Samhain (Halloween) there is an ancient custom whereby if you keep near a church porch at midnight, you may see a procession of torches pass by, indicating the actual people in that parish who are doomed to pass away soon. However, there is always the possibility that you might see your own death, so this practice is not to be encouraged. In the case of the well-known folk tale, one man saw a fairy funeral pass by one Samhain and, peering into the ...

... appearance long there. The tale ... after telling his neigh... bours about his ghastly experience, ... he was found the following day having expired in his bed with no obvious cause of death.

In the case of one's own fetch, it is more commonly an apparition that appears to convince those left strongly about. There seems to be a psychic energy that ... is thought form though the memory of emotion, enabling the fetch to communicate one has ...

ACKNOWLEDGEMENTS

Art Directors and TRIP Photo Library/ the following photographers.

© Annie Anderson: Pages: 109, 147 right
© Steve Austin: Page: 188.
© Phil Babb: Page 153.
© Martin Barlow: Page 110.
© Joan Batten: Page 216.
© Frank Blackburn: Pages 123, 147 left,
© Tibor Bognar: Pages 138, 177, 178, 185, 200, 203,
© Allen Brooks: Page 201.
© Twink Carter: Page 34.
© RS Daniel: Page 214.
© John Farmar: Page 213 right.
© Mike Feeney: Page 137.
© Mark Finnes: Page 205.
© Brian Gibbs: Pages 191, 213 left.
© Fiona Good: Page 224.
© David Hastilow: Page 151.
© Douglas Houghton: Page 27.
© Jan Isachsen: Page 180.
© Mary Jelliffe: Pages 15, 215, 217, 219,
© Tom Mackie: Page 40.
© WR Matthew: Page 207.
© Jim Merryweather: Page 208.
© NASA: Page 77.
© Edward Parker: Pages 220, 223.
© Françoise Pirson: Pages 143,
© Helene Rogers: Pages 2, 3, 5, 6, 8, 9, 12, 13 right, 18 right, 20, 21, 22, 23, 24, 25 both, 32, 36 right, 37 all, 39 below left, 43, 44, 50 both, 51, 52, 53 both, 54, 56 right, 57, 58, 59, 60, 61 both, 62, 63, 65 left, 66 right, 67, 70, 71 both, 74, 75, 76, 80, 81, 82, 86, 90, 91, 93, 94, 95, 96, 98, 112, 113, 114, 115, 116, 120, 121, 122, 124, 126, 129, 145, 152, 154, 156 below and above right, 157 below right, 158, 159 both, 160 both, 162, 164, 165, 170, 171, 172, 174, 190 both, 196, 222, 254, 72, 84.

© Robin Smith: Page 181.
© George Spenceley: Page 194.
© Jack Stanley: Page 195.
© Jane Sweeney: Page 88, 218, 221
© Th-foto Werbung: Page 47.
© Peter Treanor: Page 226.
© Joan Wakelin: Page 228.
© Liam White: Page 156 above left.
© Stuart Taylor: Page 183.
© Trip: Page 55.
© Constance Toms: Pages 48, 65 right, 78, 212, 225 left.
© Adina Tovy: Pages 187,
© Bob Turner: Pages 69, 108, 148, 150, 197, 199,
© Terry Why: Page 4, 79,

Diane Canwell & Johathan Sutherland: Pages 30, 34 both, 130, 135 all, 136 both, 140 all, 141, 175 right,

© Art on File/CORBIS: Page 244.
© Bettmann/CORBIS: Pages 225, 236, 240, 241, 242.
© Kevin Flemming/CORBIS: Page 238.
© Thomas A. Heinz/CORBIS: Page 237.
© Angelo Hornak/CORBIS: Page 239.
© Lee Snider/PhotoImages/CORBIS.
© Ed Young/CORBIS: Page 234.

Library of Congress: Pages 10, 11, 13 left, 14, 16, 17, 26, 31, 36 right, 42, 64, 66 left, 87, 182, 184, 227, 230, 231, 232 both, 233,

National Park Service: Pages 45, 46,

Kevin Oateiy: Page 18 left, 22, 35, 119, 131, 132, 133, 134, 146, 155,

Regency House Publishing Ltd: 28, 56 left, 99, 100, 102, 103, 104, 106, 107, 117, 118, 125, 144, 157 above, 166, 167, 168, 211, 225 right,